Volume XXXII: NUMBER ONE
2007

Contents

Erratum:
In volume Thirty-one, Number Two, in the article "Pushing Through Boundaries of Inner Space" by Claudia Luiz, an editing error created an erroneous citation. The paragraph that begins at the bottom of page 164 and the paragraph following it should read:

Meadow (1991) writes about this condition, "Both analyst and patient feel at least good and at times euphoric. The required oceanic state means that the analyst will not experience reality; it is a state in which ego functions have no immediate role and judgment and perceptual functions are temporarily suspended" (p. 101).

A prohibition, however, soon arrived. Mr. M got caught by the librarian—who, familiar as she was with psychoanalysis, suggested that he discuss with his analyst how he should be borrowing books. Mr. M showed up at his session in a state of extreme agitation, anxious and enraged. He was not sure he could stay in the room, and he could not take the couch.

Modern Psychoanalysis

The editors invite submissions of articles to MODERN PSYCHOANALYSIS. Manuscripts should be typed, double-spaced, on one side of 8½ ×11-inch white paper, or as a word-processing file on a CD-Rom or a 3½-inch disk. Hardcopy submissions should be in triplicate with a SASE. Footnotes and bibliographies must conform to the style of this journal. The editors should be informed, with the submission, if the article has appeared or has been submitted elsewhere.

MODERN PSYCHOANALYSIS, the journal of the Center for Modern Psychoanalytic Studies, 16 West 10th Street, New York, NY 10011, is published semiannually. Individual subscriptions are on a yearly basis: $53.00 per year. Institutions: $60.00. Write for foreign rates.

ISBN 978-0-9790972-8-7   YBK Publishers, Inc., 39 Crosby St., New York, NY 10013

MODERN PSYCHOANALYSIS is abstracted and indexed in *Psychoanalytic Abstracts* (Pa. A).

Some Thoughts on the Countertransference Resistance of the Psychoanalytic Supervisor

MIMI G. CROWELL

In analytic training and practice the role of the supervisor, the author maintains, is as significant as the role of the analyst and deserves more attention and discussion than it generally receives. Various countertransference resistances that may keep the supervisor from working effectively with the supervisee are examined, and some of the sources of these resistances and the problems they may cause in the relationship between supervisor and supervisee are discussed.

Although much has been written about psychoanalytic supervision (Fleming & Benedek, 1966; Levy & Kindler, 1995), little is to be found on the difficulties of doing supervision itself and the countertransference experiences of the supervisor. One reason may be that for some, taking on the role of supervisor is viewed as a sort of ascendance. When psychoanalysts graduate from their analytic institutes, they spend many years in practice before being accepted as training supervisors. As students they were expected, as part of their application for graduation, to demonstrate competence to practice without the interference of personal problems. Of course they often continue in analysis and in supervision and recognize the value of both. Still, when they become supervisors themselves, they may feel the need to deny their own continued difficulties as a way to reassure themselves that they are up to the task.

Even though we have spent our professional lives recognizing and utilizing our countertransference feelings with our patients, when it comes to supervision and our supervisees, it seems that we may lose this focus. We struggle daily with the challenge of giving up an agenda rooted in our own history in order to help our patients to become aware of their own psychic realities and personal desires. These struggles are also required in the supervisor/supervisee relationship, but are often not acknowledged or studied sufficiently. We are comfortable with the commitment to finding ways to liberate motivation and desire in our patients; we check ourselves when we find that we are becoming interested in manipulating the patient to have or not have certain feelings with us or when we become involved in focusing on the patient's outside life and what he is or isn't achieving outside the treatment room. We willingly relinquish our need to be seen as authorities on what is true or real. One would hope that this would also be an important perspective for the supervisor to take in regard to her supervisee. Surely, most supervisors would disavow any wish to foster a situation with the supervisee in which he feels that the supervisor has all the answers, knows what's right and true in regard to his patient, or that the supervisee must learn how to be an analyst by trying to model himself after the supervisor, in theoretical stance or technique or both. I am not referring here to the transferences that supervisees form to their supervisors—after all there is in every teacher/pupil relationship the likelihood that an idealization and a natural dependency will emerge (or that the resistance to those feelings will complicate the experience in a different way). What I am attempting to address is the resistances that lie within the supervisor to recognizing her own difficulties in working in this capacity.

In the endeavor to think through some of the problems encountered by the supervisor, it is useful to refer to Spotnitz's (2004) distinction between countertransference and countertransference resistance. He reminds us that countertransference feelings per se are not necessarily problematic; it's only when these feelings are avoided or misused that they become resistances. Accordingly, my focus in this paper is not on any feelings experienced by the supervisor toward the supervisee since none of the feelings have to cause any particular difficulty. I am concerned, instead, with feelings that for any number of reasons the supervisor is resistant to bringing into consciousness or studying more deeply.

The responsibility of the analyst in relation to the patient is to help the patient to communicate progressively, less and less encumbered by his own resistances to feeling and knowing himself. But what is the job of the supervisor in relationship to the analyst? And how does the supervisor evaluate whether or not the supervision is going well? In a 1972 lecture, Spotnitz, in presenting his view, said that the task of the supervisor is to focus on the resistance of the supervisee to working intuitively with the patient. The supervisor isn't particularly interested in teaching the supervisee how she herself would treat the patient, but rather in how the supervisee is resisting working successfully with the patient. The source of resistance may lie in ignorance (lack of information or experience) or repression (inability to use intuition). Ignorance can be handled successfully by giving instruction (although this in itself can have its disadvantages since information from the supervisor can lead to suppressing creativity in the supervisee). However, helping a supervisee use his intuition and himself as a therapeutic instrument can only be handled in analysis or supervision.

Finding the right balance between instruction and the facilitation of self-discovery can be difficult. It is generally held that the supervisor should be most interested in teaching the analyst how to conduct analysis and not in making sure that the patient is making progress. Michaels (1998) maintains that patients can be helped without analysis ever occurring, but the job of the supervisor is to teach analysis and not to do psychotherapy. Others would put it that our role as supervisors is to help the supervisee to resolve whatever blockages may be occurring within him that prevent him from seeing the patient clearly in order to understand the particular dynamics of the case and the transference, resistances, enactments, etc., so that he can go where the patient needs to go to further the process. In other words, the focus is first and foremost on the supervisee's countertransference and possible resistances in the case, and then on more theoretical issues. If the supervisee is able, over time, to show himself to be less and less encumbered by these issues and if he reports the case in a progressively clear way to the supervisor, and a sense of teamwork develops, the supervisor considers the supervision to be a success and experiences a sense of satisfaction. But what about when things don't seem to be going well? What if the student continually loses patients or continues to have difficulty in his understanding of the case and how to use the supervision successfully with the patient?

For a supervisor as for any other operative in any field, it is often all too easy to blame a lack of success on things outside oneself. The supervisor may begin to have negative feelings for the supervisee and to see him as untalented and lacking insight or enthusiasm for doing analytic work. Or, for example, the supervisor may say to herself that this lack of clarity, feelings of failure or deadness can be attributed to induced feeling from the case itself. Often supervisees will find themselves taking this perspective as well in an effort to deny negative feelings for the supervisor or a reluctance to analyze what is going on in the supervisory process. This is not to deny the force of inductions in certain experiences in the supervision. After all, the supervisee can often be unconsciously portraying to the supervisor his experience with the patient, and in fact, this can lead to a constructive result. In addition, insufficiently analyzed conflicts within the supervisee, related to his transference to his analyst or to his institute, or to other possibly destructive aims, can contribute to a lack of progress in the supervision process.

Let us return to Spotnitz's (2004) conceptualization of the sources of countertransference resistance and see how this can apply to the supervisor as well. Three sources of trouble seem especially pertinent to the situation of the supervisor working with analytic candidates at her training institute. These are the need to be liked, the need to be right, and I would add to this the need to have the student represent herself and her supervisor in a good light at the institute. Spotnitz also lists the need not to feel hate, but this seems to me to overlap with these other sources of countertransference resistance (pp. 170–171).

We easily recognize from our own training and continued work with patients the need that analysts can experience to be liked and appreciated by their patients. In the midst of a negative transference, the analyst may come to feel defeated by the unrelenting nature of destructive urges and the lack of recognition that working with narcissism can bring. When the analyst becomes narcissistically involved in these feelings, she loses the freedom to meet the patient where he is and to accept his psychic reality. In addition, unresolved issues in her own analysis, of negativity or competition with her analyst, can lead the practitioner to attempt to give her patients what she would have liked to get from her analyst or supervisor. This certainly has more to do with the analyst's negative transference than any real recognition of what her patients need.

How does this relate to the supervisor's inner experience? At the beginning of a supervisory relationship, the supervisor may find herself looking forward to this endeavor. Like the beginning of an analysis, it is all new, with many discoveries to be made. There may be some feeling of being honored that the supervisee has chosen her to take this voyage together and some gratification that she is being perceived as someone who is capable of leading such a journey. Along with this, the supervisor is in the presence of someone who, presumably, has the motivation to devote himself to a process that the supervisor has been engaged in developing throughout her professional life.

There may be the fantasy that, unlike many patients who enter into analysis not because they want to understand themselves but just to feel better, the supervisee wishes to understand unconscious motivation within his patient and himself. The sense of aloneness that analysts can sometimes feel with patients could, theoretically, be less acute with a supervisee who shares some of the same aims as the supervisor. There may be some wish, acknowledged or not, that this will ultimately be a collaborative experience, with satisfaction on both sides. However, along with a lack of experience, supervisees can often bring into the supervision feelings of inadequacy, envy, and competitiveness of their own, as well as the feelings induced by patients who have mostly pathological ways of processing destructivity. What they may often express is more a need for validation and admiration than an interest in the analytic work itself. This can be a source of disappointment for the supervisor. Once again, none of the feelings of either the supervisor or supervisee is a problem unless it leads to a resistance on either of their parts.

When the supervisee is expressing a great deal of dissatisfaction with either his own functioning, the patient's functioning, or the supervisor's, the supervisor may feel unappreciated and frustrated and may focus on the destructivity of the supervisee or the induction from the patient. This, in and of itself, is not incorrect since the sources of the difficulty can be multidetermined. However, if the supervisor does not also allow herself to examine her own desires in regard to the supervisee, and the origin of such desires, then a crucial factor is being ignored and may lead to a stalemate. I am not addressing whether or not or how the supervisor would discuss her feelings with the supervisee, but I am recommending that she study what she's experiencing to see what her part is in the difficulty. She can then use this awareness to reconnect with the supervisee in ways that are not encumbered by her own needs. As analysts, we do this as a matter of course with our patients.

In discussing the analyst's need to be right as a countertransference resistance, Spotnitz (2004) points out that the analyst's fear of saying the wrong thing, or feeling pressure to be theoretically correct, can take the place of focusing on the patient's need to be responded to with the appropriate emotional communication. The analyst may have a need to show her competence to the patient and to feel that the patient views her with respect. Obviously, a patient who needs to be in a negative state with the analyst and to express criticism and doubt will be a difficult patient for the analyst who is looking for reassurance and gratification rather than tolerating and investigating these expressions.

It is easy to see how this need to be right can show itself in the supervisory relationship. If the supervisor loses sight of helping the supervisee to create his own explanations for the phenomena he is seeing with the patient, and instead becomes invested in having the supervisee see the case in the same light as the supervisor, a great opportunity has been missed. This struggle can be most difficult. Clearly the supervisor has more experience, both technically and in regard to an understanding of theory. After all, this is why the supervisee is consulting with the supervisor. And the less experienced the supervisee is, the greater inclination the supervisor may have to impart information or give instruction as to what the supervisee should say to the patient. All supervisors do this to some extent, especially early in the supervision. Based on their understanding of the supervisee and what he may need in the moment to function more comfortably, both with the supervisor and the patient, there is value in this approach. However, what I am referring to here is a circumstance under which the supervisor is no longer attending to the needs of the supervisee, but is either trying to override her frustration with the supervisee (and indirectly express negative feelings) or to gratify herself with her own knowledge. The result is a distancing from the supervisee. This may sometimes be experienced by the supervisee as the supervisor's being more interested in the patient than in him, and sometimes that's true. This usually occurs when the supervisor has lost an ability to connect with what the supervisee is feeling and emotionally leaves the room. As analysts, we often see this when we become aware, for example, that we are identifying more with the spouse or child of the patient than with the patient himself. The cause is usually a resistance within the analyst to acknowledge feelings that are unacceptable both to the analyst and the patient.

Grinberg (1970), in discussing problems that may arise in supervision, mentions the risk of the supervisor's developing an omnipotent attitude in which she presumes to know and do everything perfectly. Obviously, this can be a reaction to feeling unsure and inadequate, which can arise even after many years of experience. This kind of attitude by the supervisor can also infect the supervisee in terms of how he presents himself to his patient—as someone with all the answers, as opposed to someone who will help the patient discover himself. In addition, we are reminded of Kuhn's (1971) perspective on how difficult it is for practitioners of any profession to alter their theoretical beliefs or approaches to their work. A lifetime has been devoted to a particular way of working or to a particular theory, and it is not questioned or released easily. The supervisor may harbor a desire to have the supervisee confirm her way of working and her theoretical views.

Supervisors often, in the face of what they see as a recalcitrant supervisee, find themselves saying in one way or another, "Did you not come to me in order to learn how I work? If so, try it and then see what you think." In other words, don't fight me so much. Again, this viewpoint has validity. I am only concerned here with when the supervisor becomes so enamored of her own ideas that she can no longer give the supervisee the sense that his ideas are valuable as well. In that situation, supervisees will sometimes go through the motions of trying it the supervisor's way, but in such a way that it will fail. This may happen anyway, but I have found that it takes place more often when the supervisee feels unacknowledged.

The supervisor's attitude toward the supervisee may also be related to another source of countertransference resistance: the supervisor and supervisee's relationship to their analytic institute. Supervisors can feel not only a responsibility to their supervisees to train them as best they can, but an obligation to the institute as well. This in and of itself is fine. It can become a difficulty if the supervisor begins to be preoccupied with, for example, how the student may be representing her at the institute. Students discuss cases in class and say, "My supervisor said . . ." which may or may not be quite accurate or presented perfectly in context. When this is reported to the supervisor in whatever form, there can be a feeling of alarm, rather than an interest in why the student is presenting it in this way. In addition, the student will ultimately be presenting cases to the faculty during the graduation process, and the supervisor may find herself worrying about how the student will do—will he demonstrate that he has a clear understanding of the dynamics of the case and is able to work analytically? Will he show an inclination for a theoretical framework other than that of the institute? I doubt that there's a supervisor for whom these questions never arise. Who doesn't want to look good and be acknowledged by their colleagues for a job well done? These kinds of concerns, however, when not acknowledged, may cause the supervisor to attempt to control the supervisee's point of view and way of working, and of course that works against the goal of helping the person learn how to think and create her own style. I think that, like patients that always seem to unconsciously pick up on the analyst's weak spots, the supervisee knows when the supervisor is more concerned with her own reputation than she is with the supervisee. This can lead to a sort of sadistic/masochistic dynamic in the relationship that is clearly destructive to the endeavor.

Another issue that may arise for supervisors is the competitive feelings that may exist between them and the supervisee's training analyst.

A case can frequently be made that the supervisee can unconsciously be motivated to create a wedge between the supervisor and analyst. In the supervisee's mind the supervisor and analyst may take turns being the good or the bad one. For instance, he may communicate to the supervisor that his analyst doesn't understand him or is not working successfully with him. Or he will say to his analyst that the supervisor has great skill and has helped him with some resistances that the analyst has never been able to touch. It's often not difficult to recognize this resistance of the supervisor/analysand. However, if the supervisor and analyst—they are commonly long-term colleagues—have a competitive relationship that has gone unacknowledged, the supervisor may unconsciously use this as an opportunity to undermine the supervisee's relationship with his analyst in a quest to be seen as superior—or even to take the supervisee away from the analyst as a patient.

Some supervisors have suggested having supervisees use the couch. The rationale behind this is that being on the couch helps the supervisee get more fully in touch with countertransference issues and allows the supervisee to speak more freely. It should be noted here that there are differing philosophies about how generally to deal with countertransference issues in supervision (Grinberg, 1970). Some supervisors believe that the supervisor shouldn't touch subjective countertransference issues, but should refer the supervisee to his analyst to discuss these. Modern analysts have found that if the supervisee is free to speak about everything, including subjective or objective countertransference or personal issues, he will pass this attitude on in his work with patients (Spotnitz, 1976). One could say that this is a resistance to talking about the case, but if one believes that the supervisor's job is to resolve the supervisee's resistances to working intuitively and therapeutically, then everything is grist for the mill. Nevertheless, the temptation to become the analyst to the supervisee has to be acknowledged and not acted upon. I believe the analytic profession would benefit from more open and serious discussion of this issue. At the moment it doesn't appear that this experimental practice of putting supervisees on the couch has been investigated fully enough to clarify certain near-inevitable subjective issues. For example, what process has the supervisor gone through in her mind to be as certain as possible that she is not acting on competitive issues with the supervisee's analyst—or is not in some way colluding in something treatment destructive with the supervisee?

Psycholanalytic supervision has always been an indispensable part of the training of each new generation of analysts. The intimacy of the process sustains the emotional and intellectual connection with those who have preceded us in this science and art, while the seriousness and dedication it both requires and inspires has enabled its refinement and evolution. It is my sense, based on many years of being a supervisee and a supervisor and on observations and discussions with colleagues, that this process remains one of the soundest foundation blocks of the profession. Supervisors spend a lifetime working to develop themselves as analytic instruments, knowing that this is a process that never ends, and they continue to be devoted to mentoring supervisees and to passing on an excitement and devotion to the work.

The aim of this paper is to put more focus on the challenges of supervision in order to bring them to the foreground of our thought for a moment. The hope is that the analyst who is doing supervision will pay as much attention to what is going on within her in her role as supervisor as she does in her role as analyst. A further hope is that the difficulties of doing supervision will begin to be discussed more frequently and more purposefully by those in training positions in analytic institutes.

Jonathan Lear (2003) says, in a formulation I endorse, that we are always in the process of becoming psychoanalysts (we never beome). That should always remain true, too, for supervisors and psychoanalytic educators. We should continually be evaluating this dynamic, fluid process for a better understanding of it and of our own part in it. For like psychoanalysis itself, what makes psychoanalytic supervision so attractive is that when successful it can lead, as few other systematic life processes can, to modification of character in both parties.

REFERENCES

Anderson, A. R., & F. McLaughlin (1963), Some observations on psychoanalytic supervision. *The Psychoanalytic Quarterly*, 32:77–93.

Bromberg, P. (1982), The supervisory process and parallel process in psychoanalysis. *Contemporary Psychoanalysis*, 18:92–110.

Fleming J. & T. Benedek (1966), *Psychoanalytic Supervision: A Method of Clinical Teaching*. New York: International Universities Press.

Grinberg, L. (1970), The problems of supervision in psychoanalytic education. *The International Journal of Psychoanalysis*, 51:371–382.

Kuhn, T. (1971), *The Structure of Scientific Revolutions*. Chicago: University of Chicago Press.

Lear, J. (2003), *Therapeutic Action: An Earnest Plea For Irony*. New York: Other Press.

Levy, J. & A. Kindler, eds. (1995), Psychoanalytic supervision. *Psychoanalytic Inquiry*, 15(2):147–273.

Michaels, R. (1998), Interview of Dr. Robert Michaels by Dr. Melvin
    Bornstein. The Carter Jenkins Center, Tampa, FL. www.thecjc.org
    /history.htm.
Spotnitz, H. (1972), Recording of Case Seminars. New York Academy of
    Medicine, New York, NY.
Spotnitz, H. (1976), Trends in modern psychoanalytic supervision.
    Modern Psychoanalysis, 1:201–217.
Spotnitz, H. (2004), *Modern Psychoanalysis of the Schizophrenic Patient:
    Theory of the Technique.* 2nd ed. New York: YBK Publishers.

80 Fifth Avenue, Ste 902
New York, NY 10011
mgcrowell25@aol.com

Modern Psychoanalysis
Vol. XXXII, No. 1, 2007

On Criticism and Being Criticized: Some Considerations

JUNE BERNSTEIN

How do we get our patients and students to relinquish their self-destructive, self-critical modes of operating? In attempting to answer this question, the author examines ways in which criticism is both expressed and experienced in the consulting room and in the classroom. Numerous case examples provide insight into the dynamics associated with giving and receiving criticism.

Part of Spotnitz's genius was forgoing interpretation, which is a form of criticism. Apparently he was less interested in explaining things, or in telling the truth, than in saying whatever it took to enable a person to function optimally. With the recent interest in showing what part of the brain lights up under various conditions, the time has probably come to find out what happens when a person is criticized by someone he cares about.

The interesting thing is that the idea of education is so tied up with telling students what they are doing wrong, presumably so that they can correct it. One has to go back to the Socratic method to teach without telling someone what he's got wrong. It seems intuitively a shortcut to let the person know what mistakes he is making, but every time I try it, real progress in understanding gets stymied. Now why should this be?

I suspect that most analyses that get anywhere have moments where the patient feels criticized. Even Spotnitz, after an ego-syntonic period where the patient feels at one with the analyst, uses interventions like ego-dystonic joining and the toxoid response. It is probably true that when the criticism has a therapeutic purpose it comes across differently from when it seems to be aimed at improving the product rather than at helping the person.

Expressing Negative Feelings

What is so enjoyable about giving criticism? For our patients, especially those who bottle up aggression, criticizing the analyst can resolve a major resistance and also, paradoxically, bring them closer to loving the analyst. We also may enjoy criticizing others because we can have the pleasure of actively inflicting on others what we have had to endure passively. Freud (1920) describes this in "Beyond the Pleasure Principle." Kohut (1972) maintains that we all have an unconscious desire to inflict a narcissistic injury. Many of us have a strong desire to "put down" someone who is displaying a trait (perhaps one that we have, or have given up) of which we disapprove or who has attacked or humiliated us.

Being a therapist is, on some level, a tacit license to point out what the patient is doing wrong in the interest of helping the patient, but the most effective therapists seem to forgo the temptation of criticizing in favor of studying and learning what enables the patient to actually operate most successfully. What moves patients forward seems to have little to do with informing them of the truth about themselves. In "The Maturational Interpretation," Spotnitz (1976) describes how a therapist gives a patient a brilliant interpretation, following which the patient thanks him, says goodbye, and is never seen again (pp. 43–46).

Why do parents criticize their children? This seems to be such a universal phenomenon that it may be worth considering it an inevitable part of everyone's experience. The ability to withstand criticism and not be devastated by it is probably an outcome of successful individuation. A person who can hear criticism and not be merged with the criticizer can say, "That's my mother (or my boss, or my friend)." A mother who is narcissistically identified with her child will express self-hatred through her criticism of her child. It is possible that the most vicious criticism is inflicted on the people with whom we are closely identified.

In doing treatment, the negative narcissistic transference is welcomed by modern analysts because it gives the patient an opportunity to discharge (and perhaps be rid of) his negative self-feelings, at least to voice them and make them conscious enough to reject them. The self-criticism of the narcissist may come across as criticism of the analyst, the family, the government—anything or anyone in the environment.

Patients (and even students in a class) often seem refreshed and energized after voicing their negative feelings. In fact, the most negative position a patient or student can take is to refuse to express negative feelings. One seminar I taught was seriously disrupted by a student who was in the grip of a corrosive hatred of the school and of me and who refused to speak. To speak might have meant that some of her rage would be dissipated, and she was taking no chances on that. She needed to hate something outside herself. A positive transference means giving all of one's feelings, including the negative ones.

I have heard the idea expressed that if a patient can dish it out, he can also take it. I have one patient who is endlessly critical of almost everyone she encounters, but is very wounded by the negative reactions she gets. Any effort to mitigate her view of the malevolence of others or to explore what she does to provoke it results in her feeling so misunderstood that the continuation of our relationship is threatened. She becomes distraught and angry and accuses me of hating her, protecting others at her expense, and being sadistic and defensive. She seems to consciously attack other people and to unconsciously attack herself.

A student at the Center for Modern Psychoanalytic Studies who repeatedly indirectly attacked the instructor and other students was baffled and devastated when another student pointed out how negative he was. This suggests that even the most critical student may need to be protected from criticism.

I have discovered that almost any negative impression one gets of how a patient functions will be received more constructively if it is put as a description of how the patient punishes himself rather that as how he is being hateful to others. A patient who is constantly dissatisfied with every aspect of his life was told that criticism was his method of attacking himself and depriving himself of pleasure. On a deeper level this is true although the induction was to feel critical of the patient. It often takes a heroic effort to say something therapeutic rather than to say something negative that seems emotionally justified.

There is undoubtedly some pleasure in being able to "tell off" another person. Unfortunately, this pleasure comes at a price. Being critical does not make friends or attract people to an analyst's practice. Analysts themselves sometimes find it hard to accept criticism. They are better able to accept criticism from sick patients than from people they respect or from patients who are high-functioning. There is a noblesse oblige in accepting the criticism of an obvious inferior that fades when working with an equal.

Criticism in the Training Process

Originally the training at the Center for Modern Psychoanalytic Studies (CMPS) contained no critical feedback. Students wrote whatever they wished in their logs, and no comments were made about what was written; they also read whatever they wished since there were few reading assignments. Process notes were the first writing requirement beyond logs, and a final paper on any psychoanalytic topic was necessary to graduate although a student could elect to graduate as a psychoanalytic psychotherapist and not write one at all. As CMPS developed, there emerged a wish that, in addition to excelling clinically, graduates be more sophisticated in psychoanalytic theory, history, and other schools of thought. Grades other than pass or fail were introduced, reading lists were developed, and candidates were evaluated on their ability to understand and write about psychoanalysis. None of this seems too out of line for a training institute, but it does mean that some students fail to make the grade, and that situation represents a significant change in the original practice and vision of modern psychoanalysis.

The reality principle requires that in running a state-accredited institution standards have to be met that may be beyond the reach of certain students. How does this turn of events affect our view of ourselves? How do we convey to certain students that their work does not meet the standard? It's back to the question of what to do about criticism. Is it possible to educate or change someone without ever being critical?

A recent graduate, whose final presentation met with tepid approval and who was hurt by the response she got, told me about a professional meeting where the speaker asserted that he had the best voice teacher in the world because the teacher wanted him to be perfect. She was still trying to master her feelings about the reception she got and was hoping it was because the faculty thought she had talent and had wanted her to be perfect. There have been a number of times when students presenting for graduation were asked to come back and present again. This rarely if ever proves to be a therapeutic experience. The recent graduate in this case did not want to think ill of the faculty or of herself, so she arrived at an explanation that protected the faculty and did not embitter her. Others have used the negative experience to justify total withdrawal from further contact.

However, we may discover that some people do not function well if we are too easily satisfied—they may feel that we do not have high aspirations for them. Some people are flattered if you want to teach them what you know; for others teaching them anything is a narcissistic injury because they should have known it already or because it means you are establishing that you are superior to them and asking them to submit to castration. (This is reminiscent of Freud's [1937] finding that in men, [and probably in women too], the refusal to accept the cure from the analyst, "the masculine protest," is the final, bedrock resistance). For some people the whole learning process is a narcissistic injury. It is not unusual for supervisees to lament, "Why didn't I think of that?" if the supervisor makes a suggestion. One supervisor used to reply, "Because then I'd be out of a job."

Students may also be critical and intimidating toward instructors. They may find modern analytic techniques in the classroom offensive. One student, who informed me privately at the beginning of class that she had to leave early, was furiously angry when I raised the issue of students' requesting permission to arrive late or leave early. (Actually, there had been a number of such requests.) She felt this was a private matter, which she had told me not to bring up. I was supposed to follow her contact.

Another, a new student, was unable to accept the process of exploring the lateness of another student. She believed I behaved unethically since I didn't know the student's psyche and might have caused a public decompensation. She wanted me to apologize, and she reported me to the authorities. She spent the rest of the semester refusing to participate and seeming to suffer. Her critical stance destroyed any enjoyment she might have had in the class and compromised the enjoyment of others. Being critical may serve to protect a person from self-criticism but seems to seriously hurt the criticizer by removing what might be sources of gratification. The student involved clearly had a good mind and would probably have relished engaging in the class discussions.

These episodes raise the question of whether we have an implicit agreement to treat students in exactly the same way we treat patients. Can we teach people to be analysts by never exploring matters they haven't agreed to discuss? How do we meet expectations that we will deliver information without engaging in classroom process (for those who want to remain disengaged) or "join" everyone in the class without regard to academic content. One possibility is to separate the analysis from the training by asking students not to take classes with their analysts. Practical considerations sometimes make this impossible although I did make such an agreement with one patient when we realized that taking classes with me put too much of a strain on our analytic relationship.

Working With the Criticizer and the Criticized

In treatment and in life, how do we work with people who always feel criticized and attacked or who are critical and attacking of us and/or themselves? An even more challenging problem: How do we work with the person who is acting as if he or she can't stand us but is saying nothing about it? The aim in such a case would be to get the person to talk about it. The person who is openly critical or complaining about being criticized is at least giving us a chance to work with him. How to work with him may require much thought and supervision.

One such patient of mine began to suffer an increase of physical symptoms and to miss sessions when I tried to explore what she might be doing to provoke so much that was wrong in her life. This made it clear to me that however miserable her life appeared to be it could get worse. I followed her instructions on how to treat her and found that her symptoms improved, and she attended her sessions regularly if I dispensed with any comments that were not supportive. She needed to be hostile without receiving any hostility in return because, she declared, her hostility was unconscious, while anything I might say was conscious and, therefore, under my control. What she wanted was what Yonata Feldman, a Russian-born supervisor and instructor in the early years at CMPS, called *"varmth and ahf-fection."* The more I could get in tune with and support her, the more we liked each other and enjoyed the sessions, and the more she thrived.

Another person I worked with had a long history of making himself (and those who cared about him) miserable. His way of succumbing to the death instinct was to destroy any pleasure he might take in being alive. He resisted success in love and work and criticized everything in his life, including me and the analysis. (He had many positive and enjoyable qualities as well, but this repetition was ruining his life.) I was tempted to tell him how destructive he was when it occurred to me that instead of being critical I could express compassion for how he was ruining his life by belittling everything about it and not allowing himself any satisfaction. Perhaps he needed permission to enjoy himself. For the first time in a long analysis during which he could never commit to the goal of getting better, he seems seriously interested in the possibility of giving up misery in favor of enjoying himself.

One student, whose conscious purpose was to make sure that he was "on the same page" as others, constantly revised, amended, or improved on anything said in class by the instructor or fellow students. He seemed to be aware of the effect he was having but baffled by it and very hurt by the group's negative reaction. In such cases there seems to be a concealed wish to be killed. It can be difficult to work with situations where students inspire negative feelings. This is a perennial and never completely resolved problem in our classrooms. Teachers vary in their ability to act therapeutically with students who inspire criticism or who are critical of them.

What about the person who is critical of himself? Meadow (1974) gives an example of responding to a patient's self-attack by saying, "You're the worst person I've ever had to put up with" (p. 82). Students in my classes are shocked by this intervention. In a discussion on working with suicidal patients, many were afraid that such a response would lead to suicide. A possible modern-analytic explanation is that if you agree with what the patient says, he doesn't have to keep arguing for his point of view and can entertain another position. The patient may feel he has been heard and can move on. As long as he hasn't been heard and acknowledged, he has to persist.

When Spotnitz called someone a bitch, the person could feel understood and accepted. Spotnitz could convey that being a bitch was perfectly okay with him. If it was okay with him, it could be okay with the patient. Some patients need to accept who they are. It is astonishing how often people want to be what they are not. One patient appeared unable to get married because he couldn't fall head over heels in love with someone and be sure he wanted to spend the rest of his life with her. However, it wasn't in his character to live up to the popular idea of romantic love. He had to get to know and accept who he was—a person who operated with uncertainty and ambivalence. That's not a terrible way to be; it's just not what's expected of the guy in a Hollywood romance.

Sometimes it seems that accepting ourselves allows us to accept our patients, students, friends, lovers, parents, and children. The man just described even managed to get married! Most patients attribute whatever has gone wrong in their lives to the critical or uncaring attitudes of their original objects. Parents either didn't care or were critical. In the present, wives, husbands, bosses, professors, colleagues, and others carry on the negative tradition of criticizing or not appreciating sufficiently. People with the most amazing successes harbor feelings that they are not acknowledged or appreciated. It seems astonishing that everyone criticizes him- or herself by being dissatisfied.

People tend to criticize others especially for traits they have renounced, like greed, showing-off, envy, grandiosity, negativity, or miserliness. They want to be perfect, and they want those they associate with to be perfect too—generous, kind, appreciative, altruistic, and object-oriented.

For a narcissistic person, and for many seemingly normal people, acknowledgement that they have ever done anything wrong or mistaken is unacceptable. Depressed people may say they have done something wrong—but the idea is so intolerable that it makes them sick. It would seem that to achieve mental health we have to know that we make mistakes and forgive ourselves. How does analysis bring that about?

In the modern theory of technique a period of mirroring and joining and exploration of contacts may be followed by more daring interventions as the patient and her repetitions become better known to the analyst. Ego-dystonic joining, like Meadow's "You're the worst person I've ever had to put up with" may succeed the initial positive period of ego-syntonic joining. Spotnitz's toxoid response, in which the analyst exposes the patient to the kind of communication that led to his overreacting in the past, is cautiously introduced to see if the patient can sustain sanity in the face of frustration. There is a gradual growth in the person's ability to know and accept himself and to tolerate criticism without feeling it means he is totally worthless.

"Do unto others as you would have them do unto you" may be completed by adding "Do unto yourself as you would have others do unto you" because others pick up and act on your feelings about yourself and will treat you as you unconsciously believe you deserve. So we better understand ourselves because even though we don't, others will.

Every kind of failure is probably a form of self-attack as well as an attack on the critical object. How do we get our patients and students to relinquish their self-destructive, self-critical modes of operating? Is it only by being better objects than the original ones? By never suggesting they might do something better themselves? By helping them to feel good about themselves? I'm not sure that Dr. Freud would approve. He was a great believer in the power of the truth. He was also a great believer in the use of tact. It looks like we just have to keep slogging along with our interminable analyses to give people time to "say everything" and not to hate themselves for the things they say or for what we say to them.

REFERENCES

Freud, S. (1920), Beyond the pleasure principle. *Standard Edition.* London: Hogarth Press, 18:3-64.

Freud, S. (1937), Analysis terminable and interminable. *Standard Edition*. London: Hogarth Press, 23:209–253.

Kohut, H. (1972), Thoughts on narcissism and narcissistic rage. *Psychoanalytic Study of the Child*. Vol. 27. R. S. Kris, A. Freud, M. Kris, & A. J. Solnit, eds. New York: Quadrangle Books.

Meadow, P. W. (1974), A research method for investigating the effectiveness of psychoanalytic techniques. *Psychoanalytic Review*, 61(1):79–94.

Spotnitz, H. (1976), *Psychotherapy of Preodipal Conditions: Schizophrenia and Severe Character Disorders*. New York: Jason Aronson.

16 Gerlach Place
Larchmont, NY 10538
junebernstein@optonline.net

Modern Psychoanalysis
Vol. XXXII, No. 1, 2007

The Joy of Violence

EUGENE GOLDWATER

Although helping professionals may have a theoretical understanding of violence as the expression of an innate destructive or aggressive drive and as a reaction to frustration or humiliation, they rarely appreciate its positive appeal. This contribution elucidates the appeal of violence as in every way equivalent to that of sex. Illustrative historical, contemporary, and clinical material is offered. Culturally and clinically, the control of violent impulses must be approached in the same manner as the control of sexual impulses. Some examples of appropriate educational and therapeutic interventions are described.

Discharge into acts of violence is always accompanied by pleasure. . . . Societies may want to study and further understand the pleasure taken in these destructive acts.

Phyllis Meadow (2003)

Practitioners, scholars, and students in the various fields of human services, who wish to improve "the human condition" both for individuals and for the society as a whole, face a paradox. On the one hand, through their clinical training and experience, they recognize the powerful influence of violent impulses on the behavior of individuals and groups. On the other hand, due to their personal temperament and history, they frequently fail to grasp the fundamental normality of these impulses, their enormous appeal, and the need to treat them with respect rather than reprobation if a satisfactory outcome is to be achieved. The goal of this paper is to clarify the roots of violence—not simply as a reaction, or a defense, but as an essential part of the human

The author appreciates the assistance and support of Linda Gochfeld, Denise Hall, Risha Handlers, Robert Mehlman, Jennifer Troobnick, and Joan White.

personality; to consider the resistance to understanding violence on the part of helping professionals; and to suggest appropriate approaches to the problem of violent behavior through educational (preventive) and maturational (therapeutic) interventions.

A particular focus of what follows is the comparison of violent feelings and behaviors with sexual ones. "Sex and violence" are frequently bracketed together as the most common foundations for popular entertainment. Yet while many of us in the helping professions—health, education, and the like—have no trouble enjoying, or at least understanding the enjoyment of, sexual pleasure, we may feel quite differently about violence, even in its vicarious forms. To what extent are sex and violence equivalent in character and appeal for "ordinary people" who have not chosen to be among the "angels" of society?

Prologue: Women and Violence

I will begin with some observations regarding the particular issue of violence in women—which, I propose, in no way differs from that in men.

> At a party one evening, standing near a small group of women, I overheard the words, "The way to a man's heart is through his stomach"—accompanied, to my surprise, by laughter. I looked over and was startled to see one of the women demonstrating how to thrust a knife up under someone's rib cage, on the left side, into his heart. "The way to a man's heart is through his stomach, right?!"

Although most of my material is about men, and most violence is done by men, *I do not believe that women have any intrinsic inability to enjoy violence, just as men enjoy violence.*

A hundred years ago, in "polite" society at least, there was a serious dispute about whether it was normal for women to enjoy sex. Some women enjoyed sex, many women did not, and the question was, which was normal? Looking back now, most of us would agree that this argument has been clearly resolved. Of course normal women have the capacity to enjoy sex, just as men do—even though, just like men, they may not exercise that capacity because of their personal values or personal circumstances.

But now, the same question has arisen with respect to violence. Some women enjoy violence, many women do not, and the question is, which is normal? I venture to suggest that a hundred years from now—assuming that civilization survives the next hundred years, which may well depend on our approach to the problem of violence—we will look back on this argument with the same amusement and say: of course normal women have the capacity to enjoy violence. Even though, just like men, they may not exercise that capacity because of their personal values, or personal circumstances.

> I am the leader of a folk dance band that specializes in songs from the Balkan countries and the Middle East. Like folk songs everywhere, these are very often about sex, or violence, or both.
>
> One of the singers in our group is a woman who made it clear when she joined us several years ago that she did not want to have anything to do with songs of violence. She would be happy to sing about love and sex—but not war or killing.
>
> One day we listened to a recording of an old Bulgarian folk song. Dinah immediately said, "That is so beautiful. I want to sing it!"
>
> Then we looked at the translation. The song is about a woman outlaw, Bojana, whose lover is the leader of the local guerilla band fighting the occupying Turks (a common theme of Bulgarian folk songs—it may even have been based on some true story, which of course many folk songs are). According to the song, the Turks captured her lover. Bojana strapped on her sword, and she went after the Turks, and she caught them, and she cut off all their heads and rescued her lover. And he said, "Bojana, you should be our leader!"
>
> Dinah listened to this story, and she said, "I like that! I'll sing it!"

In the past, when women were the objects of men's sexuality rather than being able to express their own, it wasn't fun. To the extent that they have come to be more in control of the expression of their own sexuality, they naturally enjoy it more. And I think exactly the same thing is true of violence. To the extent that a woman—or anyone—is the passive object of someone else's expression of violence, pleasure is lacking. True enjoyment comes from the active expression of one's own violent energy.

Disapproval of Violence

What exactly do I mean by enjoying violence? It has occurred to me that trying to explain the pleasures of violence to an audience of helping professionals and academics may be rather like trying to explain the pleasures of sex to an audience of monks and nuns! We like to think that we understand human nature very well. But I think our personal feelings about violence may interfere with that understanding.

Our moral attitude toward violence is very similar to the moral attitude that many religious fundamentalists have toward sex. They believe that sex is only acceptable under certain specific conditions—namely, within a committed, sanctioned, procreative relationship, or as they would say, holy matrimony. And outside such a relationship, everyone should abstain.

We helping professionals have exactly the same belief about violence. We think that violence is only acceptable under certain specific conditions—some of us believe that violence is never acceptable, but I think most of us would say that violence is acceptable to defend oneself against personal assault; to defend and protect the community as a whole (which of course we usually delegate to law enforcement professionals); to defend our country against attack; and to obtain food, if necessary. I think many of us draw a moral distinction between hunting and killing animals by tribespeople for subsistence and hunting and killing animals by recreational sportsmen and sportswomen purely for pleasure—just as religious fundamentalists draw a moral distinction between sex within a marital relationship, for the purpose of creating a family, and sex outside of marriage, purely for pleasure.

One of our popular organizations is Planned Parenthood, which promotes what we like to think of as the responsible enjoyment of sex. And which is anathema to religious fundamentalists.

One of their popular organizations is the National Rifle Association, which promotes what they like to think of as the responsible enjoyment of violence. And which is anathema to many of us helping professionals.

How did we get to be such puritans when it comes to violence? In my own case, which I think is not atypical of helping professionals, I believe it was a combination of my experiences as a child and my experiences as a professional.

I was brought up in a home where violence was not permitted. I was never hit. On the rare occasions when I hit someone else (usually my older sister), I was simply restrained. Violence was also not permitted at the school I attended. There was no bullying there that I can recall. I was never in a fight. I never learned how to attack someone. I never learned how to defend myself against attack, either.

When I was 16, I enjoyed strolling in a popular park near my house. One summer I encountered a tough kid who began harassing me whenever I went there. It was minor, but I had the distinct impression that if I didn't deal with it, it would get worse. One day, I approached him, extended my hand, and introduced myself. I'm not sure who was more surprised—he or I—but he seemed happy to make my acquaintance. After then, whenever I saw him, I greeted him in a friendly manner and exchanged a few words with him. My only intention was self-preservation.

Although my solution to this threat was purely intuitive, in retrospect I think I must have sensed that this boy lacked *connection* and *self-esteem* and that his bullying behavior simply reflected his pathetic attempt to correct this situation. (I have presented these themes—the basic needs for connection and esteem—in previous papers [Goldwater, 1989, 2004], and they are further developed below.)

As a child, I had almost no exposure to so-called "violent entertainment" on television. It seemed like quite enough to me at the time! But by today's standards, it was minimal. When I got a little bit older, I did begin seeing some violent movies that I enjoyed. I was also very impressed by how much other people enjoyed them. In the second of the James Bond movies, *From Russia with Love,* I can still remember the great roar of joy that filled the movie theater at the conclusion of the struggle in the train compartment between Bond and his enemy!

After my psychiatric training, I worked for some years in clinics and residential programs, where I encountered many people who were intimately acquainted with violence. But I never heard anything from these people about the joy of violence. Any more than I heard about the joy of sex! If I didn't have my own personal experience of sexual pleasure, I would never have gotten any sense of it from my patients. All they ever talked about were the disastrous consequences of sex: unwanted pregnancies, unwanted children, diseases, miserable relationships. No one ever talked about why they engaged in sex, or why they entered into these miserable sexual relationships.

It was the same thing with violence. All I ever heard about were the disastrous consequences of violence: injuries, deaths, incarcerations, anxieties, miserable relationships. No one ever talked about why they engaged in violence, or why they entered into these miserable violent relationships.

The eye-opener for me came when I went to a conference on the treatment of post-traumatic stress disorder in Vietnam veterans. Several cases were presented of people who had served more than one tour of duty in Vietnam—for which they had to have volunteered since no one was obliged to serve more than one tour of duty there. In the question period, someone said, "You've been telling us about all the suffering and horrible traumas of these people—why would anyone go back for more?"

The panel members, who were helping professionals, talked about pre-morbid personality and social inadequacy and inability to adjust to normal society and addiction to violence. But no one explained *why* someone would become addicted to violence!

Meanwhile, the moderator, who was a Vietnam veteran, was sitting there looking increasingly frustrated. Finally he took the microphone and said, "You know, it's hard to explain to someone who hasn't been there. But *combat is the greatest high there is.*"

He didn't even say the second greatest. He said combat is the greatest high there is.

The Necessity of Violence

At that time, I had already had my psychoanalytic training, and I was just beginning the study of evolutionary psychology, which attempts to explain behavior patterns and behavior potentials on the basis of their adaptive value. It also proposes the possibility that if certain behaviors aren't obviously adaptive now, in today's world, they may have been adaptive for our ancestors and hence laid down in our genetic inheritance (see, for example, Pinker, 2002).

From a survival perspective, our distant ancestors needed three basic behavioral repertories. They needed to know how to eat in order to obtain nourishment. They needed to know how to have sex—not for their own survival, but for that of their species (more specifically, for that of their genes). And they needed to know how to be violent in order to defend themselves against both predators and competitors and in order to obtain food and other essentials.[1]

How did nature ensure that our primitive ancestors—who didn't have our foresight or our cultural capacity to pass on information to each other through speech—would engage in these crucial behaviors? By making them pleasurable. They ate because it gave them pleasure. They had sex because it was pleasurable. (There's certainly no other reason why they would have had sex!) And they were violent because violence was—and is—an *intrinsically pleasurable activity.*

---

[1] Psychoanalysis, of course, investigates the impulses and conflicts that are associated with precisely these behavior patterns. My first psychoanalytic teacher, Ethel Person, quoted Sandor Rado as saying that psychoanalysis is the study of suck, fuck, and kill!

Violence as Fusion of Eros and Thanatos

Why is combat the greatest pleasure of all? Because there's an enemy.

We often wonder: why do so many people seem to need an enemy? We helping professionals love to engage in what we call "conflict resolution." But we're often frustrated by people who don't seem to want to have their conflicts resolved. They seem to love to fight! If we succeed in resolving one conflict, they find another. If they give up hating one person, or group, they find another.

Some may recall that at the beginning of the 1990s, after the collapse of Soviet communism, there was great angst in this country. What are we Americans going to do now? We've had this wonderful enemy for half a century! Are we going to find another country to hate? Another ideology? Another religion? Are we going to attack each other? (Or will we do all of these?!)

I believe that people want someone to hate for exactly the same reason that they want someone to love. It's a relationship.

Those of us who have worked with battered spouses will recognize this dynamic. Why don't they leave? Because a violent relationship is better than none. And the same applies to the batterers. Given a choice between a violent relationship and no relationship, which is the only choice that they see, they'll choose the violent relationship.

Violence can be very intimate. Thrusting a knife into a man's heart— you can't get much more intimate than that! Even just slapping someone around, or being slapped around, is every bit as intimate as kissing, or being kissed.

Consider that classic struggle in the train compartment between Bond and his enemy. What did they do first? They dined together. They drank together. They looked into each other's eyes and talked and laughed. And then they went to the compartment. And if we blacked out the screen and just listened to the sound track, I wonder if we would be able to tell if they were having a fight to the death . . . or great sex! *Great violence, like great sex, fuses Eros and Thanatos.*

There's an old Irish joke—I don't know why Irish, but that's the way it was told to me. What's the greatest thing in the world? To have sex with someone you love. What is the second greatest thing in the world? To have sex with someone you don't love.

It's the same thing with violence. What's the greatest thing in the world? To kill someone you hate. What's the second greatest thing in the world? To kill someone you don't hate.

Killing someone you don't hate is what we often call "senseless" violence. For example, the notorious 2002 sniper attacks in the Washington, D.C. area, which were perpetrated by two men who shot people at a distance from their car, at random. We call this senseless because we don't understand violence that has no ultimate survival value, such as defending ourselves or obtaining food. We don't appreciate the enormous *intrinsic pleasure* of violence.[2]

If the best thing is killing someone you hate, and the second best is killing someone you don't hate, is there a third best? As helping professionals, we know that there is. Individuals who can't—or don't want to—kill, or hurt, either someone they hate, or someone they don't hate, can direct the violent impulse inward, against themselves. They can cut themselves. They can kill themselves.

It's the same as with sex. If you can't find someone to love, and you can't, or don't want to, have sex with someone you don't love, you can always direct the sexual impulse inward and masturbate.

Carrying this one step further, there is a fourth option. Suppose we don't want to have sex, or violence, with someone else, or with ourselves. What else can we do with all those energies and impulses? We can direct them towards things. Or we can direct them towards people in a symbolic way. Instead of the battlefield, we can compete with other people on the playing field—or in the office. We can cut down trees and build houses. We can love truth and hate ignorance. We can have a "war on poverty." Psychoanalysis calls this *sublimation*. Society calls it *education*.

Sublimation can bring us almost all of the pleasures of direct drive discharge: excitement, relationship, pride, power, creation, destruction. Education is the process of showing people how to direct the drives and energies that otherwise would go into impulsive sex and violence, in such a way as to be of constructive benefit to themselves, and their society.

Sex and Violence

The Joy of Sex	The Joy of Violence
Excitement—Sensation	Excitement—Sensation
Relationship—Intimacy	Relationship—Intimacy
Pride—Glory	Pride—Glory
Power—Control	Power—Control
Creation	Destruction

[2]One of two men arrested for a similar series of murders in Phoenix, Arizona in 2006 was reported to have referred to his actions as "random recreational violence."

An English Soldier

People who love physical violence are not usually very good at writing about it, and the authors of first-person accounts in literature are generally less than completely frank about the nature of their experience (just like my clinic patients mentioned above). But there are exceptions.

Here are the words of an English soldier writing about his service in Afghanistan at the end of the nineteenth century:

> Except at harvest-time, when self-preservation enjoins a temporary truce, the Pathan tribes are always engaged in private or public war. Every man is a warrior. . . . Every large house is a real feudal fortress. . . . Every family cultivates its vendetta; every clan, its feud. . . . Nothing is ever forgotten. . . . The life of the Pathan is thus full of interest. (*Economist*, 2001, p. 72)

There is nothing like violence for creating "interest." *If you want some excitement, the quickest and surest way of getting it is to be violent* (Goldwater, 1994).

> Into this happy world the nineteenth century brought two new facts: the . . . rifle and the British government. . . . The convenience of the [rifle] . . . was nowhere more appreciated than in the . . . highlands. A weapon which would kill with accuracy at fifteen hundred yards opened a whole new vista of delights to every family or clan which could acquire it. One could actually remain in one's own house and fire at one's neighbor nearly a mile away . . . .

> The action of the British government on the other hand was entirely unsatisfactory. The great organizing . . . power . . . seemed to be little better than a monstrous spoil-sport.

> But towards the end of the nineteenth century [the British] began to make roads through many of the valleys. . . . All along the road people were expected to keep quiet, not to shoot one another, and, above all, not to shoot at travellers along the road. It was too much to ask. (*Economist*, 2001, p. 72)

It's a lot of fun, shooting at travelers! But it's not only the tribespeople who love violence—it's the soldiers too.

> The Political Officers who accompanied the force . . . were very unpopular . . . [one] was much disliked because [he] always stopped military operations. Just when we were looking forward to having a splendid fight and all the guns were loaded and everyone keyed up, [he] would come along and put a stop to it. (*Economist*, 2001, p. 72)

Almost half a century later, England was at war. And the war was going very badly. The German armies had overrun much of Europe, and they were poised to invade England. In this desperate situation, it became clear that the country needed a leader who *loved to fight*. That man was the same soldier who, as a youth, had written the account quoted above. His name was Winston Churchill, and here is what he said in a great radio address:

> We shall go on to the end, we shall fight in France, we shall fight on the seas and oceans, we shall fight with growing confidence and growing strength in the air, we shall defend our island, whatever the cost may be, we shall fight on the beaches, we shall fight on the landing grounds, we shall fight in the fields and in the streets, we shall fight in the hills; we shall never surrender. (Peterson, 1954, p. 780)

Did he *enjoy* giving this speech? According to an eyewitness, immediately after delivering these stirring words, which thrilled and inspired people around the world, Churchill put his hand over the microphone, *smiled* at the people standing next to him in the studio, and said, "We'll hit them over the head with beer bottles—that's all we've got!" (Peterson, 1954, p. 780).

Peacetime Europe has witnessed the emergence of English "football hooligans" who devote themselves to bashing opposing teams' fans over the head with beer bottles. I think at heart, Churchill was a hooligan!

A German Artist

Churchill's enemy was a man named Adolf Hitler. Unlike Churchill, Hitler had no interest in war or violence as a young man. He was, by all accounts, a rather timid, mild-mannered fellow. Charitable—no trace of the anti-Jewish sentiment that was quite prevalent in his surroundings. Some of his close acquaintances were Jewish. He was a bit moody, with a tendency to depression at times. Overall, his personality was pretty typical for an artist—which was all he ever wanted to be! (Rothschild, 2002)

He was so set on being an artist, in fact, that he moved from his home town to Vienna with the specific intention of enrolling in the Academy of Fine Arts there—even though the application which he had sent in had already been rejected.

Hitler had talent. He actually supported himself, after a fashion, for a couple of years selling the watercolor drawings that he made of various scenes, especially buildings. He had an interest in architecture and liked to make elaborate drawings of buildings. But he wasn't satisfied with being a sidewalk artist. He aspired to greatness. And he was sure that when he applied to the academy the second time, in person, they would accept him. He assumed that the first time they had just made a mistake.

In retrospect, I think we can all agree that they did make a mistake, a terrible, terrible mistake. And they made it again. They rejected his second application. After that, Hitler knew that he would have to achieve greatness in some other way.

But he never lost his interest in art. Even after he became one of the most powerful men in the world. Even in the final days of his life, holed up in his underground bunker, Hitler made elaborate drawings of the great cities that he dreamed of building. Over the ruins of the great cities he had destroyed.

> I had a patient once who reminded me a little bit of Hitler. He told me—many times—about how, when he was in high school, he had shown some of his drawings to someone who said, "Those are really good! You should be in the art class!"
>
> So he asked to be in the art class. But he was a special education student, and he was told that the art class was not open to special education students. Special education students were supposed to spend all of their class time studying "the basics."
>
> Thirty years later, he still *burned* with the frustration and humiliation of that rejection. Holed up in his apartment, he made elaborate drawings (which he showed me) of great battles between himself and the world.

I don't think this man could ever have been a Hitler. He was slow, and he didn't have the gift for public speaking that carried Hitler to power. But I do think that, given the right circumstances, he might have become a sniper.

Do I believe that art can substitute for violence? Yes, I do. And I believe that *art is basic.* If the mission of education is to show people how to direct their instinctive sexual and aggressive energies so as to benefit themselves and society, then *the arts are basic.*

An American Ghetto Youth

Nathan McCall (1995) has provided us with a contemporary description of the experience of violence, which some of us may find more relevant to our day-to-day work.

Carrying a gun did strange things to my head. Suddenly I became very much aware that I had the power to alter the fate of anybody I saw. The greatest power on earth is the ability to give life. *The next greatest power is the ability to take one. . . .* [italics added]

I was walking home by myself from a girl's house when the Cherry Boys [a gang] and some others spotted me and came charging my way. . . . I had the equalizer, and I wasn't scared. I waited until they got within twenty yards of me, drew the gun, aimed, and fired several shots into the crowd, *bam! bam! bam! bam!* They dove to the ground and then scattered like flies. It made me feel powerful to be able to scatter a crowd like that. (pp. 72–73)

For most of my life, I could not understand the allure of power. I knew of course that some people like power. People will kill for power. People will have sex for power.

Early in my career, I directed several drug and alcohol treatment programs, where I had the power to tell people what to do and to hire people and to fire people. I had some pride of accomplishment there, but the power aspect just didn't excite me. I never could understand what exactly is so special about power.

Then, about 10 years ago, I and some friends decided to start the dance band that I talked about earlier, and they appointed me the leader of the band. This was not something that I had asked for. In fact, they didn't even consult me about it. I just found out about it one day when our drummer was introducing me to someone, and she said, "This is our leader." That's how I found out that I was the leader!

One of the functions of the leader is to start off the band in performances. So, after we had practiced for a few months and had started playing for dances, I would be the one to raise my hand. And everyone would look at me, and I would count: "One, two, three, *and!*"

POW!!! There would be this tremendous explosion of sound, everyone working at their instruments, people dancing—and I thought: *this* is what power is all about! (To take some items from the chart above: Excitement! Sensation! Relationship! Control! Glory!)

Here is a later scene from McCall (1995):

Sensing that a rumble was about to jump off, people started crowding around. I saw my buddy Greg in the crowd, looking nervously at Plaz's boys, counting heads . . . .

Moving close enough for me to smell his breath [N.B.: When else do we get close enough to people to smell their breath?!], Plaz poked a finger in my chest. . . . "I'll kick your ass . . . !"

In one swift motion, I drew the gun, aimed it point-blank at his chest, and fired. *Bam!*

A tiny red speck appeared on the dingy white T-shirt he wore. He fell backward. His arms flew skyward and he dropped to the ground, landing on his back. As soon as they heard the blast, his boys scattered. Everybody around us ran for cover. I walked toward Plaz, *looked into his eyes* [italics added], and saw something I had never seen in him before. Gone was the fierceness that made him so intimidating all those years. In its place was shock. And fear. It was more like terror.

In that moment, I felt like God. I felt so good and powerful that I wanted to do it again. I felt like I could pull that trigger, and keep on pulling it until I emptied the gun. *Years later, I read an article in a psychology magazine that likened the feeling of shooting a gun to ejaculation. That's what it was like for me. Shooting off.* [italics added]

I stepped closer and raised the gun to shoot Plaz again, when Greg came up from behind me and called my name. "No, Nate! You don't wanna do that, man!" He carefully pulled the gun from my hand. (pp. 118–119)

Now that is *love*. This fellow, at great risk to himself, saved his friend from life in prison.

Violence brings out intense feelings: Love. Loyalty. Drama. There's *nothing like it*.

The carnival grounds . . . had turned chaotic. People ran screaming everywhere. It was like one of those movies where a monster is trampling through a city and everybody is running, hollering, fleeing for their lives. It made me feel powerful and light-headed, seeing hundreds of people scattering because of something that I'd done. (McCall, 1995, p. 119)

It reminds me of playing for dancing. Over the years, my band has played a couple of concerts for people sitting down. It's boring. The real excitement is watching everyone *move*.

The performing arts have a reputation for being even better than the fine arts as a sublimation for violent tendencies. (An elementary school principal I once interviewed, who had made a policy that every child in his school was required to play an instrument, told me flatly that children who play musical instruments do not develop behavior problems!)

I was confused about what to do next. . . . Greg asked me, "You got a ride?"

We hopped in his car and drove off. When we got out on the main street, he said, "Where you wanna go?"

I realized that I hadn't thought about that. *Where do you go after you've shot somebody?* In all the stories I'd heard . . . it was never clear what [people] did after they shot or maimed someone. There was nowhere else to go but home. I said, "Take me to the crib, man." (McCall, 1995, pp. 119–120)

It sounds like the practicing phase, where the child goes out, does his thing, and comes back to mommy! In this case, his stepfather was at home and took him to the police station without any fuss. He wasn't thinking about *consequences.*

". . . the guy your son shot, was rushed to the hospital. They're operating on him. . . . If he dies, we're going to have to charge your son with murder."

The word hit me like a sledgehammer. *Murder?! On TV westerns,* when people got shot they just tied a handkerchief around their arm and went on about their business. . . . *Plaz wasn't supposed to die.* (McCall, 1995, p. 120; italics added)

Impulse, Intent, and Consequence

How do we make sense out of this? He shot him in the chest. What does he mean, he wasn't supposed to die?

Well, it's the same thing with sex, right? People have sex. . . . *Pregnant? What do you mean, you're pregnant?!* People have sex, and they *forget* that there are consequences.

He shot this man in the chest, and he *forgot* that if you shoot someone in the chest, they might die! But then—why did he shoot him in the chest? Because he wanted to be able to *look into his eyes and see terror.* Because he wanted to watch everyone *scatter!* Because he wanted the glory of saying, *"Look at what I've done!"* It was all about the *sheer joy* of the experience.

Now, of course, as therapists, we can say, "But maybe he also had an unconscious desire." People don't want to get pregnant—but they also do want to get pregnant. This man didn't want to kill his enemy—but he also did want to kill him.

Emotional education is what people need in order to understand *all* the things that they want—not just the one that's first and foremost in their mind at the moment, but *all* the things that they want, so they can sort them out and decide what they *really* want. To put it another way: if they know all their feelings, then they can decide which feelings to act on and which not to act on.

In order to do that, of course, people need to have a knowledge of *consequences*—long-term side effects, as it were. The joy of sex has the *side effect* of creating life—which may or may not be our intention, but most certainly is nature's intention. The joy of violence has the *side effect* of destroying life (or creating death, if you will)—which may or may not be our intention but most certainly is nature's intention.

We are the ones who need to teach people about consequences. We parents, we teachers, we clinicians. They're not going to learn it from TV westerns! Which is unfortunate because, for many children right now, *television is the primary educator of behavior and morals.*

> I saw a young man who told me that he was getting in trouble for hitting people. I asked him, "What sets you off?"
>   "If someone says something I don't like, then I hit them."
>   "Why is that?" I asked.
>   "That's what you're supposed to do!"

He didn't say, "It makes me angry" or "I want to punish them." He said: *"That's what you're supposed to do."*

> He had already told me that he came from a non-violent home. It wasn't an abusive home. So I asked, "Where did you learn that?"
>   He said, "That's what they show on television!"

Although one rarely hears about it in the mainstream media—for obvious reasons—there is overwhelming evidence showing that television programming (not just advertising!) affects people's behavior in the real world, and that violent entertainment (certainly including film violence, as well) contributes to actual criminal violence (see, for example, Bok, 1998).

Will we need the equivalent of another temperance movement to convince the public that the exposure of children to repetitive vicarious violence, just like their exposure to real physical violence, is potentially addictive, dangerous to their well-being, and destructive to society?

Violence Education

I think that violence education is every bit as important in school as sex education. It appears that educating children realistically about sex doesn't make them more likely to engage in it—just the opposite, it makes them more cautious about it. This is not by telling them that sex is dirty and you shouldn't do it. It's by telling them that sex can be a joyful experience, but it can also have painful consequences. I think we should give them the same message about violence. Telling them that violence is bad and you shouldn't do it will be just as counterproductive as it is for sex. Teaching them that violence can be a joyful experience, but it can also have very painful consequences (for all parties), I believe is the most realistic approach to educating people about violence.

What should *parents* be doing to educate their children about violence?

When my son was two years old, we lived in an apartment building where there were many small children who played together. There was another toddler, named Ned, who had discovered that if he walked up to another child and pushed him, that child would topple over. He thought that was great fun. I was there one day when he pushed over my son, Daniel, and Daniel lay on the ground, crying, and Ned laughed, and Ned's mother laughed. And I wanted to kill them both!

But I didn't. I thought, how can I do something about this? I didn't have any immediate answer, so, as any parent does when they don't have an immediate answer, I thought back to my own childhood. I remembered that I had not been bullied or picked on very much even though I had (as I mentioned previously) no idea how to defend myself. Because, if someone picked on me, I got annoyed, and if they picked on me long enough, I got angry to the point where I felt that I was going to have to attack them even though I had absolutely no idea what that would consist of. But then they always backed off! Which is why I was never in a fight.

So I thought: maybe if I teach Daniel how to attack, then he won't have to actually do it. After all, I didn't want to make him into a bully, either. So that evening I got down on the floor with Daniel, on my hands and knees, and I said: "I'm going to teach you how to play a game called FIGHT. This is a very simple game. It's just pushing and hitting. There is one very important rule, which is that you can only play this game with someone who wants to play. If they don't want to play, you can't play it. However, it's very easy to tell if someone wants to play it because they'll start playing it with you. And if they start playing it with you, then you can play it with them. So now push me, and I'll fall over." Daniel pushed me, and I fell over, and I said, "That's right! That's just what it's all about!" We practiced his pushing me and my falling over, and then I said, "OK, now I'll push you, and you fall over!" And I pushed him, and he fell over, and I said, "Yes, that's the way to do it!" We practiced pushing each other over, and we practiced punching each other, and we had a great time.

And Ned never pushed him over again. In fact, which was more surprising to me, Ned stopped pushing over the other children, too.

About five years later, our daughter Sharon was four years old. She was in a preschool, and she started off the year having a great time. But a few months later, we noticed that she didn't seem to be as happy. When we asked her what was the matter, she said that a boy named Norman had been coming over to her and hitting her.

Now, this was a school with a teacher who was responsible for what happened in the class, and we could have gone to the teacher. But I wondered if what I did with Daniel would work with Sharon. So I got down on the floor with Sharon, on my hands and knees, and taught her a game called FIGHT, which she was only to play with someone who wanted to play, but if someone started to play it, then she would know that they wanted to play, and she could play it with them. I told her that it was just pushing and hitting. But I gave her another rule because four-year-olds are bigger than two-year-olds: I told her that she could hit the other person anywhere except in the face or in the penis (if they had a penis).

We pushed each other over, and we punched each other, and we had a great time. A few weeks later, I asked Sharon, "What's been happening with Norman?" She said, "He stopped bothering me."

I have a follow-up to this story. In June 2002, the school that Sharon had been in for this preschool program 22 years previously had a big celebration, and they invited everyone who had ever attended that school, and their parents. We were there with Sharon, and at some point, I noticed a tall, handsome young man, whom I didn't recognize at all, hanging around her. He seemed very taken with her. Later on, I asked her, "Who was that fellow?" She said, "Do you remember Norman?"!

Let's Get Clinical

In several previous papers (Goldwater, 1978, 1990, 1994), I have written about clinical approaches to impulsive and violent patients. The focus of this paper is more descriptive and theoretical. However, it seems appropriate to follow up on the above formulations with two specific clinical suggestions that flow logically from the arguments given above and that I have found useful in my own clinical work. The first of these has to do with what should always be the first priority of clinicians working with dangerous individuals: insuring their own personal safety.

The natural response to a potentially violent person is fear, and fear has an essential protective effect. Awareness of one's anxiety sometimes is an important reminder, and in some cases, the first indicator of danger. But should this fear be concealed or revealed? Conventional wisdom says that if an impulsive and dangerous person "smells fear," it will further stimulate the impetus to violent behavior. In my experience, the exact opposite is the case. I have found that frank acknowledgement of my fear, not only to myself but even, as appropriate, to the patient, defuses the tension and disarms the patient.

First, he feels less threatened himself. We must not forget that the natural reaction of many, if not most, persons with violent histories is one of fear and loathing toward whomever they perceive as having any power over them. Second, he now enjoys a relationship in which he has "won" respect, and therefore has no need to assert his dominance further. From the perspective of the impulsively violent individual, being regarded with respect satisfies the wish to "get even" with someone who, in the transference, is likely to be seen as powerful and dangerous (Goldwater, 2004).

Just what is "appropriate" depends on how close to consciousness the violent impulse is.

Therapist: Rather than holding your drink, could you put it on the table there?
Patient (smiling): Are you afraid I'm going to throw it in your face?
Therapist *(previously unsure why he was feeling uneasy)*: I definitely am!
Patient (laughing): All right.
Patient: If anyone says anything I don't like, I just lose it.

Therapist *(quite sure why he's feeling uneasy!)*: What sort of things set you off?
Patient: I don't know. Just anything that I don't like!
Therapist: I have some things to ask you about, but if there's anything at all that you'd rather not talk about, that's fine.
Patient: All right.

Note that these interventions are contrary to the suggestions of Liegner (1977) to use "facilitating" (reflecting) responses in a first-interview situation. In my experience, individuals who are prone to acting on violent impulses do not react well to what they perceive as unnecessary frustration. In general, impulsive patients—unlike anxious, depressed, or psychotic patients—need to begin with relatively gratifying therapeutic encounters in order to become engaged in the therapeutic process (Goldwater, 1994).

My second clinical suggestion is about joining the patient. How is it possible to validate and reinforce the feelings behind impulsive violence when the actions under consideration are at the least frightening and, at the worst, criminal and morally abhorrent? The answer, I believe, lies in appreciating the pleasure of the *fantasy* and knowing that by modeling the enjoyment of the fantasy, the therapist not only creates the conditions for a therapeutic relationship, but also helps begin the maturational process of separating fantasy from action.

> A young teenage boy with a history of learning problems was brought to my office by his parents because he had been setting fires. He sat slumped and silent while they described his misbehaviors and recalcitrance. When they were finished, I asked them to leave me alone with him.
> Some years previously, my own office had been in a building that was destroyed by a fire-setter, so I knew that I would have to make a "leap of faith" to join this boy's suffering. I took a deep breath. "Fires are really exciting, aren't they?" I asked.
> He looked up, surprised: "Yeah, I guess so. . . ."
> "Can you tell me about some really good fires that you've seen?"
> He was off and running.

In this case the dilemma of the therapist actually approximated the dilemma of the parent who is the target of the impulsive child's violence, yet needs to empathize with the child. The subsequent course of treatment included focusing on the importance of enjoyment, accomplishment, and camaraderie, all of which had been sorely lacking in this boy's life.

Another patient was easier for me to join because of some of my own personal experiences and sensitivities.

> A young woman was in therapy for "rage attacks" in addition to other impulsive behaviors. After several months of therapy, she felt sufficiently in control to attend a family gathering, despite some trepidation. She was seated at a table eating when an older female relative whom she despised suddenly scolded her for not being more mature.
> "I didn't punch her," she told me. "I didn't want to do that."
> "Why not?" I asked. "She disrespected you in front of all those people!"
> "I had a fork in my hand, and I did think of stabbing her. . . . Then I noticed that everyone at the table was looking at me, like they were expecting me to do something and wondering why I wasn't. So I looked at them, and I said, 'Well, I guess my therapy must be working!'"

The therapist here is the good object. But instead of this "splitting" leading to other objects becoming the targets of the patient's rage, the therapeutic relationship has satisfied the frustrated need for connection—and respect—and reduced the pressure on other relationships.

(Rapid behavioral improvement may of course represent a "transference cure." Permanent maturational growth may require the development and analysis of aggressive and negative transferences.)

Summary

People who have either not experienced violence or have only experienced it as recipients rather than as agents may fail to appreciate the excitement and joy that violence—exactly like sex—can provide. Violence may (again, just like sex) be encouraged or stimulated, in childhood and later, by external impressions or occurrences, such as violent models of behavior and frustrations of the fundamental needs for connection and esteem. Trying to overcome these internal and external stimuli by treating violence as inherently pathological or evil makes no more sense than does treating sex as inherently pathological or evil. For those of us who would like to diminish violence and violent behavior in the world around us, in those we love, and in our clinical work, reasonable approaches include:

1. Psychological joining;
2. Emotional education;
3. Alternative channels for physical, creative, and destructive energies (sublimation); and
4. Alternative paths to obtaining self-esteem and the respect of others, while maintaining the connections we all crave.

Addendum

The following is a verbatim account (only the child's name has been changed) taken, with permission, from a reader's response to an early draft of this paper. It illustrates my theses so well that I see no need to add any comment!

Ten years ago, my five-year-old darling daughter started kindergarten. Oh how she loved riding the school bus. Every morning she happily boarded the bus and every afternoon that beautiful smile greeted me as she bounced off it. And then one day the smile was gone. It seems a seven-year-old red-headed monster child decided to taunt and tease my little Noreen. He was relentless and she did not fight back. The joy of riding the bus was gone for her. She now cried before school, and she descended the bus steps at 2:00 pm sobbing and running into my arms.

I went to the school and talked POLITELY with the school shrink, the bus driver, and the Principal. I put in a formal official complaint (three complaints and the child would be removed from the school bus). I was not violent. I was civilized. They told me the child would be talked to. I thanked them non-violently and then went home and binge ate.

Two weeks passed. Nothing changed. I felt murderous rage as Noreen would step off the bus crying, hurt, and humiliated. I went back to the school shrink and this time I was not so polite. But I was yet to be violent. He told me I had to understand that the ginger-haired little boy came from a bad home, and I should try to understand that. I said that I was very sorry for the little boy but that wasn't really my problem—my problem was the abuse of my daughter. I filed a second formal complaint. They now brought in the parents and I was telephoned later and told my daughter wouldn't have this problem again.

Two days later my beautiful darling angel stepped off that bus, collapsed in my arms sobbing, and guess what? I BECAME VIOLENT. Without thinking further I got on the bus. The bus driver was upset. I ignored him. I marched to the back of the bus to find the red-headed little boy cringing in his seat beside the window. I lifted him straight into the air by the front of his shirt. He was terrified. I put my face as close to his as I could and whispered—yes, whispered—but with such venom and anger I hardly recognized myself. I calmly but dangerously told him that if he ever so much as looked in my daughter's direction again or spoke to her or about her in any way, I would drag him off this bus and break his fucking neck. (I never use the word "fuck" and I still wonder why sex entered this attack.) I asked him then if he understood that I would kill him. He didn't answer me. I tightened my grip around his shirt and tried to kill him with my eyes. He was terrified. He nodded "yes" to me. I violently dropped him back in his seat. I stomped off the bus with the bus driver saying something to me about my inappropriate, illegal action. I told him to "fuck himself." Another sexual reference.

I went into the house with my daughter and burst into tears. But you know what? I had a thought. And the thought was: "Wow—I'm not hungry." It's one of the few times in my life I remember specifically the absence of hunger. It was an odd sensation. I also felt tremendous power and JOY when I thought about it and reiterated the story to my extremely shocked mother (with whom I lived and who was herself a very violent person).

Guess what? The problem was solved. The big dog won. Unfortunately, I realized violence works. Two days later my Noreen exited the bus with a grin from ear to ear—pony tail bouncing along with her happy skipping. I felt a sense of joy too, knowing that from now, if I needed to use violence to protect myself or my daughter, IT WORKS.

Now here's where things get strange. The little red-haired boy always was near the bus window when I'd pick up my Noreen, and he always stared at me. I stared back with a neutral stare. One month later, he tentatively lifted his hand and "carefully" waved to me. I waved back and smiled at him as well. By the end of the school year, every day the little ginger-haired boy, whom I threatened to kill (and meant it), was waving enthusiastically to me, and every day I waved back enthusiastically at him. He never again spoke to my daughter, but he and I somehow were still in a relationship—a relationship based only on one encounter of extreme violence.

REFERENCES

Bok, S. (1998), *Mayhem: Violence as Public Entertainment*. Reading, MA: Addison-Wesley.

Economist, December 22, 2001, 361(8243):72. Quoting Sir Winston Churchill, *My Early Life*. London: Eland, 2000.

Goldwater, E. (1978), A model for understanding and treating the impulsive patient. *Modern Psychoanalysis*, 3:173–196.

Goldwater, E. (1989), What do men want? *Modern Psychoanalysis*, 14:75–87.

Goldwater, E. (1990), Male sexuality and male aggression. *Modern Psychoanalysis*, 15:225–236.

Goldwater, E. (1994), Impulsivity, aggression, fantasy, space and time. *Modern Psychoanalysis*, 19:19–26.

Goldwater, E. (2004), Getting mad and getting even. *Modern Psychoanalysis*, 29:23–36.

Liegner, E. (1977), The first interview in modern psychoanalysis. *Modern Psychoanalysis*, 2:55–66.

McCall, N. (1995), *Makes Me Wanna Holler: A Young Black Man in America*. New York: Vintage Books.

Meadow, P. W. (2003), Drives, aggression, destructivity. *Modern Psychoanalysis*, 28:199–205.

Peterson, H. (1954), *A Treasury of the World's Great Speeches*. New York: Simon and Schuster.

Pinker, S. (2002), *The Blank Slate: The Modern Denial of Human Nature*. New York: Viking.

Rothschild, D. (2002), *Prelude to a Nightmare: Art, Politics, and Hitler's Early Years in Vienna, 1906–1913*. Williamstown, MA.: Williams College Museum of Art.

9 Forest Edge Rd.
Amherst, MA 01002
egoldwater@oit.umass.edu

Modern Psychoanalysis
Vol. XXXII, No. 1, 2007

Wrestling with Destiny:
The Promise of Psychoanalysis

LUCY HOLMES

Can psychoanalysis help us change our destinies? This paper consid-
ers the various ways in which destiny is linked to the repetition compul-
sion and how psychoanalysis can, indeed, help the individual reshape
his future. Utilizing some of the latest findings of neuroscience, the
author describes how electrical impulses originating in the most prim-
itive areas of the brain are processed by higher levels of the brain and
converted into language, strengthening the cerebral cortex and giving
the patient control over his own destiny. Some of the resistances to giv-
ing up destructive patterns are described and illustrated with clinical
examples.

Do we believe in destiny? In the myths that are most meaningful to
us—the fairy tales we cut our teeth on, in Shakespeare and the
Greek myths, even in the novels of lesser and greater merit that entertain us on the beach in the summer, destiny is very real. In "The
Sleeping Beauty," a curse is put on a baby princess by a slighted and
wicked fairy. She predicts that the baby will be pricked by the needle
of a spinning wheel and fall down dead; and though this curse is soft-
ened by a kinder fairy who decrees a long sleep rather than death, nothing can prevent the princess's fate from being enacted. Indeed, the
father's frantic efforts to change the story by banning all spinning
wheels only helps bring about his daughter's destiny. The same is true
of the myth of Oedipus. Oedipus's father maims him and casts him out
to die to forestall the horrible fate, patricide and incest, predicted by the

© 2007 CMPS/*Modern Psychoanalysis*, Vol. 32, No. 1

oracle, but his efforts only hasten the inevitable. Romeo and Juliet are "star-crossed"; despite their goodness and beauty, they are doomed to their tragic end.

In all of these stories, there is a common denominator: *not knowing.* Sleeping Beauty didn't know what a spinning wheel was, and so when at last she had occasion to see one, she had to touch it. Oedipus was ignorant of the fact that his adoptive parents were not his biological ones, and so he didn't realize he was murdering his father and marrying his mother. Romeo didn't know that Juliet, like Sleeping Beauty, was not dead, but asleep, and so he killed himself. Can knowledge save us from malevolent destiny? If we can be courageous enough to confront what we don't know or, more importantly, what we don't want to know, can we win control over our own destiny?

Certainly, this is the promise of psychoanalysis. Like the myth makers and the poets, psychoanalysts believe that destiny is real—though we call it by the name of repetition compulsion. We believe that there is a dark power in every human being that unchecked can propel a person against his will to a tragic end. Though we design our own destinies with our repetitions, the true architect of our fate is the unconscious.

Destiny and the Repetition Compulsion

Freud (1924, 1927) conceived of destiny as relating in the unconscious to the power of the parents, particularly the punishing father. The early father is projected onto the external world and called fate. When we were children, the father punished us when we were bad, and since we all go on being bad, we arrange to insure that we will go on being punished. This is what makes us associate destiny with angry gods and tragic ends. In "Beyond the Pleasure Principle," Freud (1920) hypothesizes a compulsion to repeat that is more primitive, more elementary, and more instinctual than the pleasure principle, which it overrides. Working in the service of the death instinct, this compulsion seeks to return the organism to an earlier state of affairs.

LaPlanche and Pontalis (1973) describe the repetition compulsion as an ungovernable process originating in the unconscious. The subject deliberately puts himself in distressing situations, thereby repeating an old experience that he does not consciously remember. As Freud (1920) states, what is not remembered will be repeated. The repetition compulsion, in the final analysis, expresses the most general character of the instincts, their conservatism. This is the concept of the inertia of living matter: its disinclination to abandon an old position in favor of a new one. Human beings like to maintain the existing state of things, even if this state is very painful indeed. So our fate becomes an automatic and impulsive repetition of unpleasurable situations.

Bibring (1943) felt that patterns of coping that we acquire at the very beginning of life are retained and reproduced over and over in a way that determines our destiny. A formative influence on an instinctual drive is brought about by a traumatic experience that influences the course and aim of the instinct. Repetitions occur when traumatic experiences have not been assimilated. If we have had to endure a lot of excessively traumatic stimuli in our early life, we use our adaptions and defenses to bind these stimuli by anticathexis. Instincts tend to cling to primary or intense experiences and to follow the way paved by these experiences, irrespective of pleasure or pain. As we continually repeat the traumatic situation, the toxins are discharged in fractional amounts in a way that makes them more bearable. In repeating dangerous situations, the unknown becomes familiar, with a decrease in emotional cathexis. Looked at from this perspective, the repetition compulsion has both a repetitive and a restitutive tendency. One of my female patients who has been divorced three times said, "I keep marrying my mother, hoping that I can change the story and finally get a happy ending with her." This repetitive tendency is a function of the id, while the restitutive hope for a happy ending is the work of the ego.

Freud said famously that anatomy is destiny, and he wrote extensively about how a penis, or the lack of one, can have profound effects on human beings. I (Holmes, 2000) have studied and written about how girls use the internalization of maternal and paternal objects in the same way that boys use the penis: to attain separation and mastery over powerful parental figures. All of these adaptions to being male and female occur very early in life on an unconscious level, and they get acted out over and over for good or ill as we go through the life cycle. Although women are making real gains in the working world, and men are becoming more comfortable taking responsibility for children and the home, our gender nonetheless guides us in ways conscious and unconscious toward our individual destinies.

Many human beings see fate as an expression of a divine will (Freud, 1930). They find the idea that destiny is just a monster created out of the garbage dump of a lifetime of mistakes totally repellent, and so they take solace in the idea of a god who has a plan for them on this earth. Even if that plan is to suffer and die, they find comfort in the knowledge that their pain is not their own responsibility, and if they can bear it with courage and grace, they will get their reward in heaven. How gratifying it is to feel that God exists and that we have no control! Like a child in the back seat of a car, we can enjoy the view and say, "I wonder where we're going." Reassuring as this concept is, it can also be dangerous. If you believe there's a god that guides your hand, then you have no personal responsibility for all the unspeakable acts that are carried out in god's name. The murder, torture, barbarism, and destruction that human beings have inflicted on this long-suffering world in the name of God have been with us from the murder of the early Christians through the Holocaust to all the recent acts of terrorism perpetrated by radical Islamists.

Bollas (1989) likes to differentiate between destiny and fate. He equates fate with neurosis. The person who comes to psychoanalysis with neurotic or psychotic ideas can be described as a fated person. Her symptom is the oracle predicting her doom. These unfortunate patients are interred in an internal world of self and object relations that endlessly repeats the same scenarios. They have no hope for the future; indeed the idea of a future is simply the endless repetition of the past. A glimpse into the future is a vision from fate, echoing the voice of the mother, the father, or the toxic environment that oppresses the self. This sense of fate is a feeling of despair over one's inability to influence the course of one's life.

Destiny, to Bollas, is another matter. Destiny is a positive drive, an urge to articulate our true selves. It is the creative potential in a person's life. One of the most important tasks of an analysis is to enable a patient to come into contact with his destiny, to articulate his true nature through the creative use of objects. Lacan's (1977) concept of *jouissance* (enjoyment) also embodies the idea that the individual can find pleasure in his choice and use of objects. The pursuit of *jouissance* is each person's true destiny, and if one is fortunate, if one is determined and aggressive enough, this enlightened state can be achieved. The work of analysis becomes a creative destruction of the past in order to see the potential of the future and to make a psychic investment in creating that future. When the future holds positive possibilities, destiny is no longer a matter of chance. It becomes a choice—not a thing to passively endure, but a thing to be achieved.

Gaining Control over Our Destinies

Bollas's idea of a personal destiny is an optimistic and exciting one; all of us want to help our patients go from feeling fated to feeling that they can control and savor their own destinies. So the question becomes: How do we help people get there? When we see that a patient has gotten control over her repetitions, what has happened? How has she achieved it? How have we achieved it? What have we created together in the analysis which has enabled the patient to move forward toward new and creative experience?

I have thought about this question for many years. New patients often ask me, "How does psychoanalysis work? You don't say much, and I do all the talking." They find it hard to believe that just talking can help them. My patients and I have struggled over the question and come up with lots of different answers: Psychoanalysis provides a corrective emotional experience; psychoanalysis is therapeutic in its simple essence—spending time with a person who is completely focused on understanding you, not inflicting his projections or fantasies or ideas on you, but trying to understand how you are trapped in your own inflexible fate. These ideas are among the answers or partial answers about how we can help our patients. But I have always felt there was more to learn about how psychoanalysis helps a person shape his destiny.

Exciting new work in the field of neuroscience that has led to discoveries about the brain and how it works is providing physical and scientific corroboration of the psychoanalytic theories that Freud postulated a century ago as well as the later theories of modern psychoanalysis developed by Hyman Spotnitz in the 1960s and 1970s. In 1969, Spotnitz was writing about the curative process in psychoanalysis as "the deactivation of certain neural pathways and the activation of others" (p. 99).

The neuroscientist Paul MacLean (in Restak, 1979, and Shepherd, 2005) describes the evolution of the human brain as expanding in a hierarchical pattern along the lines of three basic structures in the brain, each with "its own way of perceiving and responding to the world" (Shepherd, 2005, p. 48). These "three brains" have evolved methods of communicating with each other. Brain one, the first to evolve, is reptilian in nature. It governs mechanical and unconscious behaviors and is the seat of what we call instinct, and what Freud called the id.

The mammalian brain, or the limbic system, was the next area to develop. Wrapped around the reptilian brain, the limbic system allowed sight, smell, and hearing to operate together and created a primitive memory system. It also made the nurturance of offspring possible. Emotions are generated but do not become conscious here. The third brain, which has developed in only the last hundred thousand years, is the cerebral cortex. This center of thinking and reasoning evolved with the advent of language and is where consciousness resides. Freud called it the ego.

One of the most interesting things about these three brains is that the neuronal connections from brain one and brain two upward are a great deal stronger than those from the cortex downward. That explains the difficulty we experience in using logic and insight to change a feeling. One goal of analysis is to strengthen the cerebral cortex to free the patient from the repetitive, obsessive behaviors that are characteristic of the lower two brains. I believe this is achieved by the constant conversion of primitive impulses and feelings into words. This is similar to the goal that Freud stated for analysis: Where there was id, ego shall be.

Panksepp (1998) has studied the brains of cats and rats, and one of his most important findings is that feeling is older than thought. There were emotions in the brain millions of years before there was mind to interpret them. We are used to believing that feelings are caused by events or thoughts, but that is evidently not true. Feelings arise out of neurobiological circuits in the limbic system; they are the effect, not the cause, of arousal systems in the brain. Feelings are not actually felt until they are experienced by the cerebral cortex. These circuits are inherited by the species and by each individual organism. No specific thoughts or behaviors are directly inherited, but dispositions to feel, think, and act in various ways and in various situations are. Although these dispositions do not necessarily dictate our destinies, they powerfully promote certain possibilities and diminish others.

While basic emotional circuits are among the tools provided by nature, Panksepp believes that their ability to control our destinies depends on the nurturance or lack of nurturance that the world provides. Emotional systems, like the body, can be strengthened by use and weakened by disuse.

This picture of the brain and of the origin of feelings has given me new ideas about how psychoanalysis can change one's destiny. In psychoanalysis, the contract is to "say everything." So we are constantly inviting the patient to convert into language the electrical impulses pulsing up from the reptilian brain and the feelings traveling along neurobiological circuits in the mammalian brain. In this process, we are inviting access by the cerebral cortex to those bullies, the lower brains. And, I believe, we are strengthening the young and often overpowered upper brain against the instincts and primitive feelings that are all too often acted out in the world in a way that insures a star-crossed destiny. When messages from the lower brains are put into words, instincts lose their primitive power, and feelings can be felt and verbalized, rather than acting as mandates to often destructive action. As analysis progresses, communication from the lower two brains gradually becomes data, not commands. The patient can evaluate this data and then decide how she wants to deal with it. At this point, the patient takes charge of her own destiny.

This is by no means an easy process. There are many pitfalls along the way. When patients decide to behave in ways that go against the familiar pathways of their repetitions, they may experience all sorts of terrible feelings as well as an enormous amount of anxiety. I remember a patient in a group of mine who for years had taken care of the men in the group. She had had a series of unsuccessful relationships outside the group, and inside it she compulsively mothered the men, while unconsciously feeling a lot of contempt for what she saw as their childishness and dependency, which she, in a way, had created. As this pattern became more conscious to her, she began to develop new longings. No longer so interested in taking care of the men, she developed a hunger to be loved by them. As she became able to put this new yearning into words, she induced new feelings in the men. They very cooperatively began to love her, and so we came to a point in the group where this woman took on a whole new role. No longer the caretaker, she began to be the object of a tremendous amount of masculine affection and attention. But it was interesting to me that instead of being delighted by this development, she began to feel primitive anxiety and got the idea that she had to leave the group. When the group explored this with her, all she could say was, "There's something not right about this. I don't deserve all this attention." I told her she didn't have to deserve it. "Nobody really deserves to get love," I said, "All you have to do is know you want it." Sometimes when a man in the group was talking to this woman with love and empathy, she would begin to cry, look at me in distress, and say, "Oh, my mother is going to kill me!" Anxiety about punishment and guilt always accompanies constructive change and must be worked through in the analysis.

A man I worked with described what it feels like to decide to go against your repetitions and change your destiny. He said, "When I behave in a way that is not self-destructive, I feel like I have a penny in my hand, and I release it. And instead of falling to the ground, it floats up into the sky. It's very disorienting and unpleasant."

Patients often report that their lives are not as exciting when they change self-destructive habits and find new, more satisfying objects. "I still think about Robert," a woman who had just made a new and happy marriage told me. "He was bad news with his drug use and his constant unemployment and his cheating on me, but God—he was so exciting. I think he was the love of my life." What is it that is so thrilling to many of us about these self-destructive repetitions? Why do we feel slightly bored when we find objects who so effortlessly make us happy? I think it is because the compulsion to repeat the old, sad story is fueled by the hope that this time, finally, the ending will be different. We will master the situation, triumph over it, make people who are incapable of love finally love us. What could be more exciting! It's the primitive thrill the tyrannosaurus rex must have felt when he finally grabbed the pteradactyl and ate him up. Reptilian pleasures probably are more exciting than day-to-day satisfaction. So, at some point, a conscious choice has to be made.

One of the most painful feelings involved in becoming the master of our own fate is a sense of mourning. Giving up old repetitions is often experienced as the death, or even murder, of beloved early objects. Taking charge of our destiny means saying goodbye to those objects; being happy feels like a betrayal of the people who made us and taught us, for better or worse, how to be in this world. When I first came to New York, I was in an acting class in which the teacher could get any of the students to cry by having the student stand in front of the class and wave, "Bye-bye, bye-bye," like an infant. No matter how toxic or how painful the past has been, it hurts the heart to relinquish it.

Our repetitions haunt us like the spirits in ghost stories. They cannot be put to rest until psychoanalysis solves the mystery and breaks the spell. Most people come into analysis wanting to change their feelings. Making unpleasant feelings go away is, for them, the definition of cure. But this death of feeling is not really the goal of psychoanalysis. Feelings are like weather. When fated patients come to our offices, the weather is violent and dangerous, forcing the patient to take cover and defend himself with all sorts of pathological defenses and unconscious repetitions and reenactments. As the talking cure progresses, the weather settles down a little, becomes less dangerous to the person, and finally, like the fluctuation of sun and rain, winter and summer, love and hate, or joy and grief, becomes a thing to be enjoyed.

A Buddhist yogi, Dharmaraksita (quoted in Jinpa, 2005) composed a text entitled "The Wheel Weapon Striking at the Vital Points of the Enemy." In this text, there is a reference to destiny and the very human obsession to repeat:

> Forsaking ethical discipline, the liberation path, I cling to my paternal home.
> Casting my happiness into the river, I chase after misery.
> Dance and trample on the head of this betrayer, false conception
> Mortally strike at the heart of this butcher and enemy, Ego! (pp. 152—153)

In the dance we call psychoanalysis, patient and therapist endeavor to trample on the false conceptions of the repetition compulsion, that enemy which does tend to butcher any hope for happiness or for control over our own fate. I have devoted my life to psychoanalysis because I believe it is an ethical discipline, a path to liberation.

REFERENCES

Bibring, E. (1943), The conception of the repetition compulsion. *Psychoanalytic Quarterly,* 12:486–519.

Bollas, C. (1989), *Forces of Destiny: Psychoanalysis and the Human Idiom.* Northvale, NJ: Jason Aronson.

Freud, S. (1920), Beyond the pleasure principle. *Standard Edition.* London: Hogarth Press, 23:3–64.

Freud, S. (1924), The economic problem of masochism. *Standard Edition.* London: Hogarth Press, 19:159–170.

Freud, S. (1928), Dostoevsky and parricide. *Standard Edition.* London: Hogarth Press, 21:175–196.

Freud, S. (1930), Civilization and its discontents. *Standard Edition.* London: Hogarth Press, 21:59–145.

Holmes, L. (2000), The internal triangle: new theories of female development. *Modern Psychoanalysis,* 25:207–226.

Jinpa, T., trans. & ed. (2005), *Mind Training: The Great Collection.* Boston: Wisdom Publications.

Lacan, J. (1977), *Écrits: A Selection.* A. Sheridan, trans. London: Tavistock Publications.

LaPlanche J. & J. B. Pontalis (1973), *The Language of Psychoanalysis.* New York: W. W. Norton & Company.

Panksepp, J. (1998), *Affective Neuroscience.* New York & London: Oxford University Press.

Restak, R. (1979), *The Brain: The Last Frontier.* New York: Doubleday.

Shepherd, M. (2005), Toward a psychobiology of desire. *Modern Psychoanalysis,* 30:43–59.

Spotnitz, H. (1969), *Modern Psychoanalysis of the Schizophrenic Patient.* New York: Grune and Stratton.

52 East 78th Street, #2A
New York, NY 10021
lucyholmes@nyc.rr.com

Modern Psychoanalysis
Vol. XXXII, No. 1, 2007

For the Love of Theory

ROBIN POLLACK GOMOLIN

In this paper the author discloses her passion for psychoanalytic theory. Through the presentation of case vignettes she demonstrates how theory is an essential aspect of her clinical understanding as well as her patients' therapeutic process.

I begin this paper with a confession. What first attracted me to psycho-analysis was its rich body of literature. In the earliest period of my train-ing, my interest in clinical work lagged well behind my passion for psy-choanalytic theory. At that time, what turned me on most about my patients was not my involvement in their analytic process, but how their symptoms brought to life the theories of my favorite psychoanalytic writers.

Many analysts argue that theory has no place in the analytic room, that what makes for a successful therapeutic outcome is the development of a stable, safe transference relationship through which associations, con-flicts, and enactments become available for observation and analysis. Dr. Meadow once told me that all she needed to conduct analyses was action. As I mature analytically, my appreciation for her words continues to grow. At the end of the day, it often is the analysis of behavior (as reported by patients and enacted with us) that leads to our and to their deeper understanding of unconscious motivation. There is however a caveat to this statement. How we choose to understand the action of our patients and respond emotionally is always, to some degree, informed by theory.[1]

A primary concern with theory is that if we adhere to it too rigidly, we will preconceive the analytic process of patients. Our literature is full of

---

[1] I would argue that we probably never have access to a "pure" countertransference experience since theory modifies our feelings immediately by obligating us to investigate the objective and subjective elements of the event.

© 2007 CMPS/*Modern Psychoanalysis*, Vol. 32, No. 1

advisories concerning this hazard. Hurvitz (1986) cites Michels (1981) who writes that "Different analysts with different theories can construct different analysands out of what began as the same patient and confirm their theories in the process" (p. 440). Similarly, Tuckett (1993) argues that our thoughts, perceptions, and observations can never exist separately from the theory that informs them (p. 1176). Though we aim for our psyches to be au natural during the analytic process, Rothstein (1980) suggests that we may seek cover in theory when we face the tensions of new and uncertain clinical situations. Several psychoanalysts venture further, noting that the choice of a particular theory is not simply a matter of picking a particular scientific truth. It reflects a personal truth about the analyst (Guntrip, 1975, 1996; Hurwitz, 1986; Ticho, 1982).

Though we must pay great heed to these words of caution, I firmly believe that theory always informs clinical process whether we admit to it or not. Perhaps the best way to demonstrate my assertion is through illustrations that depict how theoretical knowledge is an essential ingredient of my work. In keeping with Dr. Meadow's love of action, I begin this discussion with one of my favorite papers, Freud's (1912) "Remembering, Repeating and Working-Through."

In this hallmark paper he discusses a "special class" of experiences, occuring during early childhood, that are not understood prior to their being forgotten but are later understood and interpreted during analysis. According to Freud (1912), "one is obliged to believe in them on the most compelling evidence provided by the fabric of the neurosis" (p.149). In some cases, memories of this class may be relinquished through analysis. With regard to those that remain unconscious, Freud states, "We may say that the patient does not remember anything of what he has forgotten and repressed, but acts it out. He reproduces it not as a memory but as an action; he repeats it, without, of course, knowing that he is repeating it" (p. 150).

I get excited every time I read this passage. I think it's brilliant. When it comes to my patients and the repetitive conflicts they present, nothing feels truer than these words. During a recent session Freud's understanding entered my mind and allowed me to understand the actions of a patient in a very new way.

The Case of Jane

Jane began treatment three years ago. Initially, she claimed that she needed help managing her parents' reaction to the discovery of her bisexuality and alcohol use. Although she acknowledged a promiscuous quality to her sexual encounters and a tendency to overuse alcohol and other substances, she negated this awareness by suggesting that many college students, like herself, indulged in similar behaviors.

I quickly learned that these issues were the least of Jane's problems. She has tremendous difficulty tolerating opinions and ideas that differ from her own. She is anti-authority and defiant in extreme and self-destructive ways. I have always silently disagreed with her idea that many of her behaviors could be attributed to a delayed adolescence.

Jane is tremendously bright and capable in her chosen field of study, yet her achievements are limited by her inability to tolerate the arousals that come with mastering new material and respecting academic structure. She finds it "completely unacceptable" that professors have attendance requirements and frequently refers to them as "assholes." During sessions, she is highly animated and has frequent outbursts of rage in response to those individuals she perceives to be imposing structure upon her. "Who the fuck do they think they are?" I am often asked by colleagues who my 4:00 o'clock screamer is. Jane's hysterical cries feel like infantile and omnipotent cravings, as opposed to a rebellious adolescent surge striving for separation.[2]

In her last session prior to a lengthy summer separation, Jane revealed that she had been fired from her part-time job and that the campus police had found her near her dorm, passed out, with a large gash on her forehead.

She then revealed that this was the second time campus police had found her drunk, and that as a consequence of university policy, she was facing suspension. As usual, Jane couldn't understand why she should have to answer to anyone for her actions. With her imminent departure we had no time to analyze her need to keep me in the dark about the prior incident on campus or the degree to which she was abusing drugs and alcohol.

Several weeks prior to her return from break, I received a frantic call from Jane telling me that she had picked up a man in a bar and had unprotected sex with him in his hotel room. He had also become violent with her when she attempted to leave his room. It would be several weeks before Jane's destructive actions could be analyzed. I should add

---

[2]This diagnostic distinction occurred to me spontaneously in the moment of writing about Jane. I didn't impose a theory on my observations of Jane's behavior. My knowledge of psychoanalytic theory, as it pertains to emotional maturation, guided this assessment. Meissner (2002) states that without a theoretical orientation the analyst can make little sense of the patient's material (p. 344). I agree.

that there wasn't a theory in the world that helped me manage my intense countertransference feelings during these weeks.

Upon her return, Jane arrived at her first session distraught and enraged as she faced suspension. She presented in her usual intense way, but her hysterics somehow felt different. There was a sense of meaninglessness that had not been present before. I wondered whether my new perception was merely an artifact of my anxieties about her frantic call to me, which she had not yet spoken about. I let her continue ranting until I was certain that my perception was based on new elements within Jane's presentation. I then offered her the following comment: "It was not until you presented me with your suspension prior to the break and called me several weeks ago that I realized the extent of the risks that you take with your life. Today I began to understand what all these risks are accomplishing for you. It seems important that you destroy anything meaningful in the external world so they match how you feel on the inside." As I was finishing my comment, Jane looked at me and said, "Yes, that is right. That is it exactly. If everything out there is crap, then there is no conflict for me. Everything is meaningless. Everything is shit and I don't have to bother with living."

My words to Jane were informed by my awareness that actions articulate the unconscious, often prompting the disclosure of painful and overwhelming feeling states. Myers (1987) suggests that action can bring the patient face to face with feelings that are blocked off and is a way to restore a sense of control over them and a connection with life (p. 655). I believe this to be true for Jane. Action eased her descent into self-knowledge, which is terrifying to us both.

Jane is not the spontaneous, in-the-moment party girl she presented herself as during the first three years of analysis. In this post-action period, I am learning how dead and empty she feels on the inside and how she "came out" of this state through promiscuity and alcohol and drug abuse. I believe that her flight into action kept her from encountering a sense of meaninglessness that would have promoted an active suicidal gesture, rather than a passive enactment of an abject state that she could not allow himself to know.

McDougall (1984) writes about a group of patients "with unsuspected psychotic anxieties or extreme narcissistic fragility who disperse their affective experiences through action as a way to avoid any awareness of extreme emotion" (p. 388). Jane's high-octave presentation during sessions, her drug and alcohol abuse and promiscuity were attempts to keep strong affect states away from active cognition. It was only following their commission and disclosure that a space within her became available for the deeper analysis of her unconscious wishes.

I am equally enamored of Melanie Klein's theories on infantile mental development and early defense mechanisms. Her writings deepen
my respect for the dynamic forces that confine human beings to their
emotional and behavioral repetitions. Her descriptions focus on the
earliest stages of ego development and are vivid and original. These
provocative insights into the unfolding mind provide us with access to
its existential struggle and the defense mechanisms invoked in its attempt
to master primitive anxiety. Her conceptualization of the paranoid-
schizoid stage and the depressive position, as well as her critical attention to the psychic activities that are implicated as a consequence of the
transition from one phase to the next (i.e., the ego's integration of the
loved and hated aspects of the breast/mother, and the development of
guilt, the reparative drive, and ambivalence) are, in my opinion, gems.
I cannot imagine the study of character in the absence of these precious
understandings. The following vignette demonstrates the dominance of
the early defense mechanism of splitting in two patients.

Barbie and Ken

The patients I think of as "Barbie" and "Ken" have been in treatment with
me for six and four years, respectively. These pseudonyms come immediately to mind for them. They are not related, but their physical attractiveness, coupled with their strikingly similar symptoms and inhibitions,
seem cast from the same mold. Both are intelligent and highly articulate,
yet work at jobs they perceive as below their intellectual potential.
Despite their attractiveness, both experience great difficulty establishing
intimate relationships, and their social networks are meager. Each of
them has one good friend who possesses the same self-limiting attributes.

There have been many moments in these patients' analyses that felt
identical and left me feeling confused. Describing these moments in
supervision and writing about them now induces the same feeling, no
doubt symbolizing some aspect of these interludes. During sessions,
when speaking about interactions with bosses, co-workers, or random
people they met at social events in which they perceived the behavior
or words of the other person as demeaning, these patients reported
responding in a highly aggressive manner.[3] If words could kill, this

[3]Neither ever says he or she feels demeaned. I interpolate this missing affective link as I listen
to their stories. Both Ken and Barbie have split from the psychic space that would allow them to
be aware of this affect.

would be their unconscious intent. For example in reporting a conversation with his boss, Ken described the following interchange:

> So he was discussing his plan for the project, and he told me that he was very upset about some political activity in the region and that he planned to do something about it. When he told me what he intended to do, I said to him, "Look you moron this is how you get the job done. You hire a fucking hit man and take the guy out. Then he will understand you mean business. You don't act like some pussy if you want to be taken seriously."

While in the restroom of a lounge, Barbie saw a woman whom she believed was "checking her out." She reported the following:

> I went to freshen up and ran into this woman I used to know. We had some common friends. I hadn't seen her in a long time. I had heard that she was engaged to some guy. She was okay looking, nothing great. I could tell she was giving me the once over and was jealous of the way I looked. I said, "Stop staring at me bitch. It's not my fault I look better than you."

This type of aggressive exchange was frequently reported. The image of road kill kept entering my mind as Ken and Barbie spoke of running over human beings in their social encounters. My countertransference was filled with anxiety. My patients, however, would pass on to the next association as though nothing had happened. I controlled my frequent impulse to ask questions and studied these scenes, which over time provided me with great insight into the vulnerable psyches of these individuals.

When I understood that what was being reported was a fantasized version of a dialogue, I was able to intervene in a way that allowed for a deeper exploration of these moments. In reality, both Ken and Barbie always sat paralyzed and mute as they faced tensions that overwhelmed their psyches. This clinical example brings the following words of Klein (1946) to life. In speaking about the denial of psychic reality and the infantile ego's inability to tolerate pain and frustration she writes,

> In hallucinatory gratification therefore two interrelated processes take place: the omnipotent conjuring up of the ideal object and situation and the equally omnipotent annihilation of the bad persecutory object and the painful situation. (p. 102)

It is passages like this one, in which a theorist is able to convey the essence of psychic conflict and its remedy with such astute clarity, that make me passionate about theory. In their reporting, Ken and Barbie were hallucinating a gratifying scene that corrected their response to unbearable stimulation. The only way for them to maintain any sense of self-cohesion was to split from the virtual scene and imagine one in which their words killed off the villain who was standing in for an archaic object.

Theory has taught us that some of our patients convert psychic angst to illness. What ails them remains beyond the realm of language, confined to the primitive senses of the body private. Freud (1923) wrote that the ego is a projection of an inner surface derived from bodily sensations. "The ego is first and foremost a bodily ego" (p. 26). Other writers (Krystal, 1974; Meares, 1997; Schur, 1958) elaborated upon Freud's view of somatic phenomena as a failure or regression of ego function. Their insights help us understand that the maturation of affects is contingent upon their increasing desomatization as well as their separation and differentiation from the matrix of the body.

Elsewhere (Gomolin 2003), I have described this process as the cell division of the mind. Successful completion yields a maturing mental apparatus, one that is increasingly able to contain and manage drive energy through libidinal patterns of binding and neutralization. This physiological adjustment of drive energy marks the transition from somatic to psychological experience. Winnicott (1966) refers to the "real and insuperable difficulty" of working with patients whose organized defense keeps the somatic dysfunction and conflict in the psyche separate (p. 510). A patient in treatment with me for five years illustrates Winnicott's observation.

A Congested Psyche

Stan, a 42-year-old single man, began treatment five years ago in a state of desperation. He had been to the best doctors in Boston (and elsewhere in the United States) seeking advice about his nasal congestion. Extensive tests failed to uncover any underlying cause. Medications, allergy shots, vaporizers, vitamins, special diets, holistic treatments, acupuncture, and multiple surgeries yielded no relief. Stan gave me six months to fix him, and if I failed, he assured me he would kill himself.

Stan doesn't want to *actively* talk about the issues patients often discuss in treatment. I emphasize actively because over the years I have gotten to know quite a bit about Stan, despite his need to believe that he doesn't tell me anything. He claims that he doesn't dream and is certain that the past has nothing to do with his symptoms and that there is no point in talking about sex since he is too congested to have any! His ideas that he isn't talking and that talking is "useless" are loaded transference communications that let me know a great deal about Stan's earliest experiences of attunement.

According to Stan, he is the unluckiest person in the world. Had it not been for a sister born before him who died several days following her birth, Stan wouldn't even be in the world. His conception was a result of bad luck, and nothing has gone right since then. His parents divorced when he was three. Sunday visits with his dad were spent waiting in the back seat of his car while he and his second wife visited open houses. When his dad took him to dinner at his club, Stan recalls being left alone to eat while his father visited the tables of his many lawyer friends.

Stan's mother lured him into her overwhelming anxieties, raising him to be frightened of everything. To this day, she advises Stan how to negotiate inclement weather and the numerous other perils that he might fall victim or prey to. Fearing that discipline might "hurt" Stan, she gave him none. As a consequence, the activities of daily living overwhelm him. Given what Stan has told me about his mother's crazy, extreme behavior, it is easy for me understand why his affects must remain congested. If he could breathe, it would be with fury and vengeance. His congestion in part represents a failure in an essential ego function: the capacity to neutralize aggression (Schur, 1958, p. 132)

McDougall (1974) writes that psychosomatic symptoms tell the story of an archaic drama (p. 441). Other prominent writers agree that the transference with patients like Stan offers a reconstruction of the original infant-mother relationship: one in which the child's healthy strivings towards independence were rejected and illness and dependence were rewarded (Sperling, 1955; Savitt, 1969). Even when Stan feels good, he can't enjoy himself because he anticipates the return of his congestion. An excerpt from Stan's process illustrates this dilemma and how he continues to relive the extreme frustrations of an anxious, unpredictable holding environment.

> I had two hours of feeling good. I got excited. I just got so excited. I wanted to cry just at the thought I might be able to feel good. Lately I don't even have a safe haven [Stan used to be able to get relief from his congestion at home or in my office. In the last year he is congested in these places also.] Today I had a 50 percent day. I was happy to have half of a half day. I'm struggling to survive. The more I try, the harder it is to get better. Each day brings a new unpredictable thing. I've tried harder

than anyone I know. The harder I try, the more frustrated I am. I get stonewalled. I can't win.

During his sessions, Stan focuses on how congested and suicidal he is. On his birthday, he asked me to mercy-kill him. Yet on many occasions, I find out that he is actually doing a good deal of living. Pleasure must be had on the sly, offered in the transference that way, lest I reject his strivings towards autonomy. Stan frequently forwards me emails he receives from his mother. They reflect an extreme preoccupation with anxiety and her need to have him live a highly inhibited life, similar to her own.

Stan tells me that eight years ago he decided he had to move away from the state his mother was living in because he knew if he didn't, she would make him crazy. He immediately became symptomatic. Psychoanalytic theory lets me know that his congestion also represents an unconscious wish to remain attached to her. He, however, negates any possibility that there is a relationship between these two events and remains convinced that the etiology of the congestion is biological. Sperling (1955) sees the psychosomatic response as an unconscious bid for a continuation of a relationship that gratifies infantile needs. She also writes that the illness provides gratification. The suffering of bodily symptoms appeases the demands of Stan's punitive superego. "By releasing destructive impulses in the symptoms, he saves himself from feelings of guilt and anxiety" (p. 321).

I understood the uncanny nature of Stan's congestion well before I read the works cited above. I experienced its regressive elements in the transference and in my countertransference. Theory, however, organized my impressions into a more formal understanding of this tenacious symptom and its significance with respect to Stan's mental cohesion.

In a very recent session, as he was leaving my office, Stan said, "I think there is more of a chance that I can fix my nose than my mother." I almost fell out of my chair. I could not have appreciated the clinical importance of Stan's spontaneous association had I not read Bion's (1959) theories, most specifically "Attacks on Linking," where he writes that a consequence of hatred is the destruction of "embryonic thought which forms a link between sense impressions and consciousness" (p. 313).

Psychic Activity and Alan

Alan has been in treatment with me for seven years. His official psychiatric diagnosis is bipolar disorder. Elsewhere (Gomolin, 2002,

2005), I have described the first years of his analysis as delusional and manic. Now, more in touch with the affects that promote his flight, he frequently laments the loss of a more continuous state of mania. It was a constant "reserve of energy" that bailed him out of difficult realities.

Despite his consistent business failures and the loss of tremendous amounts of money, Alan clings to an image of himself as an entrepreneur. He remains unable to relinquish this fantasy. Each time I watch him enact his impossible dream, I feel truly humbled by the unconscious and its powerful defense mechanisms.

The total erasure from his mind of the dire consequences his "business plans" pose to his existence is better understood within Klein's (1935) conceptualization, which notes that a sense of omnipotence, based on denial, is a central feature of mania. She writes that in mania "that which is first of all denied is psychic reality and the ego may then go on to deny a great deal of external reality" (p. 161).

Lewin (1949) likens the expressions of mania to the playful wish fulfillment and dreams of a child and adds that they are bursting with an innocence, as well as an immediate need for gratification (pp. 420–421). This aptly describes Alan, who commits himself to project after project without any knowledge or preparation. For example, imagining the success he would have as a limousine driver, Alan purchased a very expensive, stretch Mercedes Benz before investigating any of the practical issues involved in such an undertaking. He was "bursting with innocence." In the aftermath of his ill-thought-out pursuits, Alan's discourse of failure replicates Klein's (1935) descriptions of denial.

His manic enactments return him to a state of profound dependency on others (wife, sister, brother, children).[4] He then becomes consumed by a seething, projective hatred. Gabbard (1989, 2000) writes that hatred is a means through which connections with primitive internal object representations can be maintained in an unforgiving manner.[5] The writings of other psychoanalysts have deepened my understanding that hatred represents a pathological attachment to primitive object impressions. Hatred is utilized to create an adjustment that ensures psychic continuity (Kernberg, 1991; Galdston, 1987; Pao, 1965). Alan's hatred is primitive, as opposed to relational.

[4]Klein (1935) describes the psychic position of the ego in relation to the object as one of extreme dependency, "torturous and perilous" (p.161).

[5]Kernberg (1991) provides an excellent discussion of how hatred condenses, organizes, and expresses within its pattern of sadomasochistic behaviors a reversal of suffering—a symbolic revenge triumph over the object, as well as triumph over a terrifying self-representation (p. 229).

My countertransference arousals testify to those archaic psychic states that Alan's mania seeks to deny.[6] Over the years, I have struggled to understand the persistence of his irrational choices, as well as the level of regression we both experience as his failures enter the treatment. I revisit these classic writings on mania regularly. They offer no magical solution; however, they do capture the psychic paradox of this patient's condition. Often, they steady me. More often than not, they deepen my emotional experiencing of Alan. Most importantly, they always form the basis of the communications I extend to him—communications that must respond to experiences that are largely perceptual and impressionistic. As theory advances my technique, I embrace its role as the guardian of a very complex process.

Conclusion

I suspect that if you have read this far, you are now fully convinced of my love for theory. Fenichel (1938) wrote that our theory summarizes the laws of human psychic activity and that the analytic process should be based upon our knowledge of these laws. Understanding the deepest layers of unconscious dynamics intellectually is a prerequisite of my clinical work. My unconscious, emotional resilience and empathy are equally central to my analytic listening. However, if I listen without theory, what sense can I make of my patients' words, enactments, or those deepest feeling states that I know resound within them?[7] More importantly, how can I be attuned to them?

There is nothing more fascinating than human behavior, and there is no other discipline whose theories have traveled the back roads of consciousness as extensively as psychoanalysis has. In our work, we have a tremendous opportunity to observe the destructive powers of the unconscious and the regenerative powers of the ego. In this age of cognitive, behavioral, and other "managed" cures, it is more important than ever that we organize our clinical observations into theories that speak to the powerful relationship between transference, talking, and the emotional growth of our patients.

[6]Those states include melancholia, the mastery of a paranoid condition based on the psychic position of the pre-ego in relation to the object, i.e., total dependency.

[7]For a wonderful discussion of this question I recommend Meissner's (2000) paper "On Analytic Listening."

A PS on Theory

If you are prone to epistemophilia, then you know that withdrawing from a discussion of theory is always a challenge—hence this *PS*. It wasn't until I read the following passage from Loewald (1978) that I understood (emotionally and intellectually) the psycho-anatomy of the preverbal period and its many implications with regard to emotional maturation and our clinical work:

> Perception, memory and reality testing, in their primitive conformations, are unconscious instinctual activities that are eventually distinguished as instinctual affective life and cognitive functions. In such bifurcation the original global functioning, although dominated and overshadowed by specialized modes of functioning, remains preserved: libidinal-aggressive elements remain ingredients of perception and memory, considered as ego functions, and constitute the unconscious motivational aspect of the latter. (p. 495)

This excerpt emphasizes that the ego, no matter how advanced it is, can never be considered an autonomous structure. It is the unconscious which forever remains the black box of human perception. When we speak of resistance, we are referring to a dynamic reluctance to collapse those partitions of the mind that separate higher cognitive function from the raw anxieties of instinctual life. For this reason alone, we understand that the human condition is best characterized as a tension state where pathology and adaptation, to some degree, always coexist.

REFERENCES

Bion, W. R. (1959), Attacks on linking. *International Journal of Psychoanalysis*, 40: 308–315.

Fenichel, O. (1938), Problems of psychoanalytic technique. *Psychoanalytic Quarterly*, 7:421–442.

Freud, S. (1914), Remembering, repeating and working-through. *Standard Edition*. London: Hogarth Press. 12:145–157.

Freud, S. (1923), The ego and the id. *Standard Edition*. London: Hogarth Press, 19:19–63.

Freud, S. (1926), Inhibitions, symptoms and anxiety. *Standard Edition*. London: Hogarth Press, 20:87–175.

Gabbard, G. (1989), Patients who hate. *Psychiatry*, 52:96–106.

Gabbard, G. (2000), Hatred and its rewards. *Psychoanalytic Inquiry*, 20: 409–420.

Galdston, R. (1987), The longest pleasure: a psychoanalytic study of hatred. *International Journal of Psychoanalysis*, 68:371–378.

Gomolin, R. P. (2002), The countertransference dream. *Modern Psychoanalysis*, 27:51–73.

Gomolin, R. P. (2003), Unpublished manuscript.

Gomolin, R. P. (2005), The death of an entrepreneur: a systematic analysis of a manic defense. *Modern Psychoanalysis*, 30:1–19.

Guntrip, H. (1996), My experience of analysis with Fairbairn and Winnicott: (how complete a result does psychoanalytic theory achieve?) *International Review of Psycho-Analysis*, 2:145–156.

Guntrip, H. (1996). My experience of analysis with Fairbairn and Winnicott. *International Journal of Psychoanalysis*, 77: 739–754.

Hurwitz, M. (1986), The analyst, his theory and the psychoanalytic process. *Psychoanalytic Study of the Child*, 41:439–466.

Kernberg, O. (1991), The psychopathology of hatred. *Journal of the American Psychoanalytic Association*, 39:209–238.

Klein, M. (1935), A contribution to the psychogenesis of manic depressive states. *International Journal of Psychoanalysis*, 16:145–174.

Klein, M. (1946), Notes on some schizoid mechanisms. *International Journal of Psychoanalysis*, 27:99–110.

Krystal, H. (1974), The genetic development of affects and affect regression. *Annual of Psychoanalysis*, 2:98–126.

Lewin, B. (1949), Mania and sleep. *Psychoanalytic Quarterly*, 18:419–433.

Loewald, H. (1978), Instinct theory, object relations and psychic structure formation. *Journal of the American Psychoanalytic Association*, 26:493–506.

McDougall, J. (1974), The psychosoma and the psychoanalytic process. *International Journal of Psychoanalysis*, 1:437–459.

McDougall, J. (1984), The "dis-affected" patient: reflections on affect pathology. *Psychoanalytic Quarterly*, 53:386–409.

Meares, R. (1997), Stimulus entrapment: on a common basis of somatization. *Psychoanalytic Inquiry*, 17:223–234.

Meissner, W. W. (2000), On analytic listening. *Psychoanalytic Quarterly*, 69:317–367.

Myers, W. (1987), Actions speak louder. *Psychoanalytic Quarterly*, 56:645–666.

Pao, P. (1965), The role of hatred in the ego. *Psychoanalytic Quarterly*, 34:257–264.

Rothstein, A. (1980), Psychoanalytic paradigms and their narcissistic investment. *Journal of the American Psychoanalytic Association,* 28:385–395.

Savitt, R. (1969), Transference, somatization, and symbiotic need. *Journal of the American Psychoanalytic Association,* 17:1030–1054.

Schur, M. (1955), Comments on the metapsychology of somatization. *Psychoanalytic Study of the Child,* 10:119–164.

Sperling, M. (1955), Psychosis and psychosomatic illness. *International Journal of Psychoanalysis,* 36:320–327.

Ticho, E. (1982), The alternate schools and the self. *Journal of the American Psychoanalytic Association,* 30:849–862.

Tuckett, D. (1993), Some thoughts on the presentation and discussion of the clinical material of psychoanalysis. *International Journal of Psychoanalysis,* 74:1175–1189.

Winnicott, D. W. (1966), Psychosomatic illness in its positive and negative aspects. *International Journal of Psychoanalysis,* 47:510–516.

1581 Beacon Street
Brookline, MA
robingomolin@gmail.com

Modern Psychoanalysis
Vol. XXXII, No. 1, 2007

Finding the Right Feeling: Objective Countertransference and the Curative Emotional Communication

PAUL GELTNER

This paper explores how the objective countertransference can be used by the analyst to determine the curative emotional communication required to resolve a resistance and/or meet a maturational need. The author delineates four different ways in which the emotional communication the analyst chooses may relate to the countertransference feelings induced by the patient. Many case examples illustrate the process the analyst may go through in selecting an intervention.

Spotnitz wasn't the first analyst to use emotional communication in psychoanalytic technique. Freud acknowledged its importance in a limited role that was subordinate to the work of interpretation. Ferenczi (1955) experimented with a wide range of emotional communications but did so in an unsystematic way that often led to a loss of control of the regression in the analysis (Balint, 1968). Other analysts, from the "Budapest School" (Moreau Ricaud, 2000), recognized the value of more disciplined emotional communication. Alexander (1925) went so far as to describe analysis as "a corrective emotional experience," and Balint (1952, 1968) defined a clear but restricted role for emotional communication with pathology rooted in "the basic fault." Winnicott

(1949) and Sechehaye (1951) both made extensive and sophisticated use of emotional communication. But Spotnitz was the first to develop a range of specific, goal-directed techniques of emotional communication and to explain their rationale within a well-developed theory of technique for the treatment of preoedipal disorders.

Spotnitz's technique (1976, 1983, 1989, 2004) is grounded in an understanding of transference and objective countertransference and is designed to resolve resistances and to meet maturational needs that have been unresponsive to traditional interpretations. A complete introduction to the modern psychoanalytic technique is beyond the scope of this paper. But it should be emphasized that these interventions are designed solely to enable the patient to consciously experience and to verbalize intense feeling states (such as hate)—never to punish, control, or humiliate. It also assumes that the countertransference is objective, which requires a painstaking study of the material to sort out subjective countertransference, which is unrelated to the patient.

For a deeper understanding of the use of these techniques, the reader is referred to Spotnitz's works cited, and further to other modern analytic writers, especially Margolis (1978, 1979, 1994), Meadow (1987, 1988, 1989, 1991), Liegner (1980, 1991, 1995), A. Bernstein (1992), W. Kirman (1980), J. Kirman (1983, 1998), Sherman (1983), Hayden (1983), J. Bernstein (1981, 1993), Marshall (1993), Laquercia (1992, 1998), Ernsberger (1979, 1990), and Weinstein (1986).

Although current orientations recognize the centrality of emotional communication to psychoanalytic cure—notably the relationalists and the intersubjectivists—modern psychoanalysis remains unique in the range of feelings it utilizes and the variety of ways that emotional communication is integrated into interventions.

But where do these feelings come from? In the course of every analysis, the analyst experiences a range of feelings about the patient. An objective countertransference is a feeling that is induced by the patient (Winnicott, 1949; Spotnitz, 1985) that is consistent with some aspect of the patient's life history.

On the other hand, a curative emotional communication is a feeling, expressed by the analyst, that resolves a resistance and/or meets a maturational need. Although a curative emotional communication is tailored to the individual patient at a specific point in the analysis, we can say in general that the curative emotional communication will be similar enough to a feeling that the patient has experienced in his past to be compelling, but different enough to be curative (W. Kirman, 1980b).

The question arises: What is the relationship of the objective countertransference to the curative emotional communication? Unfortunately, there is no direct correspondence between them. However, there are usually four possibilities. The curative emotional communication can be:

1. the same feeling as the objective countertransference
2. essentially the same feeling, but at a significantly different intensity
3. approximately the same feeling, but expressed in a different mode of relatedness
4. a completely different feeling, most often a feeling that is the opposite of the objective countertransference

The Objective Countertransference as the Curative Emotional Communication

Sometimes, the objective countertransference feeling is itself the curative emotional communication, in the sense that the analyst can communicate the induced feeling (implicitly or explicitly), and this feeling will be curative for the patient. For example, the patient tells the analyst that he got a job that is particularly hard to get, and the analyst feels admiring of the patient: the analyst's admiration is the curative emotional communication. The intensity of the feeling may have to be modified slightly—perhaps the patient is now in a position to absorb more admiration than previously, but less than the analyst actually feels—but this is usually not significant enough to change the feeling.

Here's another example: The patient describes a fight with his boyfriend. He complains that the boyfriend ran up the credit card with bills for expensive clothes even though the boyfriend lost his job and the patient, with great difficulty, is supporting him. The patient voices some anger with the boyfriend but seems to minimize its intensity with sympathetic rationalizations for the boyfriend's behavior. The analyst senses that he is not allowing himself the full intensity of his anger, so the analyst directly communicates his induced feelings: "If he were my boyfriend, I'd scream my head off until he returned every last pair of socks!" This is the emotional communication that the patient needs in order to fully feel and express his anger.

A final example: The analyst knows, from the patient's own stories, that the patient has a history of taking advantage of his friends—despite his gregarious and seemingly innocent demeanor. One day the patient casually asks the analyst whether he could borrow one of his books, and the analyst is irritated by the patient's presumptuousness. The analyst asks, with evident irritation, "Why should I lend you one of my books? I know how you take care of things." The patient, who until then has been polite to the point of obsequiousness, pours out a stream of hate at the analyst's lack of trust and generosity. The communication facilitates the verbalization of aggression that the patient had previously defended against, acting it out passive-aggressively through his irresponsible behavior. It also brings the patient's exploitative behavior into the transference where it can be worked on.

However, situations where the induced feelings may be used therapeutically are rare; more commonly, the objective countertransference spontaneously repeats the past in a non-curative and possibly traumatic way.

The Curative Communication Based on the Objective Countertransference, but Differing in Intensity

In these cases, the analyst experiences a specific feeling that must be modified significantly in order for the patient to be able to make use of it. This may occur when the intensity of the countertransference is strongly incongruent with the intensity of the content.

Let's return to the patient with the spendthrift boyfriend. But this time, the patient does not complain about him, or complains minimally, while the analyst feels so angry with the boyfriend that he really wants to kill him. However, after the analyst says, "If he were my boyfriend, I'd scream my head off," the patient defends the boyfriend or becomes anxious about getting cancer. This suggests that the emotional communication has activated the patient's defenses. In this case, the curative emotional communication might be something like: "Some people find it a little stressful when they are the primary provider, and their partner doesn't fully appreciate what that means," delivered in a confident tone with just a hint of anger largely overshadowed by sympathetic empathy. This response communicates a feeling that is in the same emotional spectrum as the first communication, but so much less intense that it seems like a different feeling altogether.

Or, the induced feeling may have to be intensified. Let's take the same scenario as above, but this time the analyst, like the patient, is only very mildly annoyed. In this case, it is possible that the patient needs the analyst to model more intense anger at the boyfriend to help him feel that getting really angry is acceptable.

The Curative Emotional Communication Using a Mode of Relatedness Different from the Objective Countertransference

Consider the following case: The patient drones on in a low tone of voice that induces boredom, depletion, and fatigue. The analyst hates it. His mind wanders; he wants to sleep; and he finds it impossible to stay on track listening to the patient. The analyst does not just feel miserable; he feels that the patient is making him miserable. His first thought is that the patient's droning is passive-aggressive—a deliberate (although probably unconscious) withholding of life-sustaining stimulation. Consequently, the analyst feels attacked by the patient and irritated at him because the patient is boring him.

How do we understand this situation? The most likely possibility is that this is a repetition of the parent's feeling. Perhaps the patient expressed his depression as crankiness when he was a child. This may have induced depressed feelings in the parent, but the parent did not recognize them as an empathic resonance with the child's depressed feelings. Instead, he experienced them as an attack on his own sense of well-being. Thus, he experienced the depression in the wrong mode of relatedness and misunderstood the child's attempt to communicate his depression. Out of irritation, he told the child to stop complaining and ruining everyone's good time, which caused the patient to tone down his complaints and adopt the monotone. This formed the basis for a repetition in which the patient continued to strive for a narcissistic emotional communication, but continually induced the parent's feeling instead. Other people experienced the patient's depressed feelings in the object mode as an attack upon their own good moods, leaving the patient to cope with his depression in isolation and feeling criticized for being boring.

What then is the curative emotional communication? The analyst knows that many people have told the patient that he is boring, passive-aggressive, and withholding and that this has always hurt him. So, the analyst is certain that communicating the irritation would be repetitive, but not curative. It occurs to him that the interpersonal picture looks different if viewed in terms of the patient's self-experience, i.e., his depression. Perhaps nobody communicates empathic understanding of the pain of the patient's depleted depression; nobody even recognizes that the patient communicates his depression by making the other person feel bored. This suggests that the analyst should try a narcissistic emotional communication based on the patient's depression. This might mean silently containing the depression and communicating an occasional grunt of agreement with the patient's despair. Or, the analyst might say, "You know, sometimes life just feels so hard and mean and boring—it's hard to even keep your head up," in a forlorn, exhausted tone. In this way, the analyst communicates the specific feeling in the countertransference—the feeling of boredom—but in a different mode of relatedness (i.e., in a narcissistic rather than object mode) than the one in which he originally experienced it.

In the scenario given, the analyst's misunderstanding of the mode of relatedness of the bored/depressed feeling was rooted in a repetition. Sometimes, however, the analyst experiences the right feeling in a non-curative mode of relatedness for subjective reasons. For example, the analyst might have a low tolerance for boredom and a propensity to experience anyone who bores him as a threat to his well-being.

The analyst might also misunderstand the mode of relatedness for theoretical reasons. For example, he has trained himself to see all interpersonal exchanges as taking place in the object or intersubjective modes; consequently, he consistently misunderstands narcissistic inductions. Similarly, an analyst might be trained to understand all countertransference narcissistically, in which case he would have a propensity to misunderstand object inductions. In either case, it is difficult to find the curative emotional communication when the mode of relatedness is misunderstood.

Emotional Communication Differing Completely from the Object Transference

Situations in which the analyst experiences the right specific feeling in the countertransference but must change the mode of relatedness occur fairly often. However, not all specific feelings can be transposed from one mode of relatedness into another. These are the cases in which the curative emotional communication is completely different from the induced countertransference.

Let's look at an obvious example: the patient has forgotten to bring the check, and the analyst's first reaction is impatience and anger. "Why can't that patient be more responsible," he thinks. "Why does he make me wait for my money? Why can't he take care of anything himself?"

The patient has recounted many stories like this: he forgets things, and people become harsh with him. So, the analyst's reaction is obviously a repetition. The analyst also remembers the patient's reactions to being criticized: he feels hurt and withdraws; or he gets angry in return, but the anger doesn't free him up either. Nothing ever changes. With this in mind, the analyst cannot see any rationale for communicating the countertransference. He doesn't think that changing the intensity will make any difference; irritation just seems to be the wrong feeling to communicate, at least in the object mode.

He then considers changing the mode of relatedness. Is it possible that experiencing the irritation in the narcissistic mode instead will yield the curative emotional communication? Thus, the analyst imagines what it would be like if he were angry with himself instead of with the patient and realizes that the patient might be angry with himself for not bringing the check. This is a definite possibility and might lead to a narcissistic emotional communication, which might be something like: "It's frustrating to forget things, isn't it? It makes you so angry at yourself." Or, "I know just what it's like. I always forget to bring checks and pay people. They get so angry. It's so upsetting!"

But what if the analyst doesn't think that will work either. The patient may need help in figuring out how to remember things. For example, the analyst might ask: "It seems like it's hard for you to remember this kind of thing. Is there a better way we can handle this? Would you prefer to mail me the check? Or is there anything that might help you remember?" Or, "Would you like to leave some checks here, and I will keep them in my desk. You don't have to worry about remembering them, and you won't fill them out until the end of each month?" In this case, the curative feeling would be almost the opposite of the induced feeling—both in feeling and in mode of relatedness.

Now, let's look at the scenario in reverse. Again, the patient forgets the check, but this time the analyst wants to help the patient to learn how to remember. However, he has tried a number of times, and it's never worked. He recalls that the patient's parents are always very "helpful" to him and realizes he may be having the same feeling the parents have.

He considers an empathic communication: "It's so frustrating to forget things like checks." But he's tried this previously without effect. Finally, he considers the possibility that both the patient's confused and apologetic demeanors are expressions of passive-aggressive defiance or hatred of the analyst, or are sadomasochistic provocations. If so, the curative emotional communication might be: "What the hell is wrong with you? Can't you remember anything at all?" The curative feeling is the opposite of the induction.

Another situation in which the curative emotional communication may be completely different from the countertransference occurs when the countertransference is strongly incongruent with the content. This situation suggests that the patient's conscious experience is strongly defended against the unconscious transference that is inducing the countertransference. In these cases, the analyst should usually contain the induced feeling, while making an emotional communication related purely to the content.

For example, consider a case in which the patient describes her daughter's sleep problems: the baby has been up crying for many nights in a row. The analyst is filled with fantasies of tossing babies in the air and letting them smash on the sidewalk. These aggressive fantasies about babies are probably related to the unconscious content of the patient's communication; however, they are strongly incongruent with her affect and her conscious experience. She describes only love for her child and expresses sadness that the baby is so upset. She also feels helpless and asks the analyst how she should handle the situation. While her concern is certainly genuine, there appears to be a defense operating against experiencing the aggression that she feels toward her baby, a hypothesis that would explain the analyst's fantasies. However, the analyst thinks that any reference to the aggression would disrupt the patient's defenses. Instead, he makes suggestions about coping with the baby's crying. Thus, he contains the aggressive feelings, which are related to the unconscious narcissistic transference, and he expresses an anaclitic communication that is related primarily to the patient's conscious experience—and is completely different from the induction.

Auto-induction: Stimulating the Curative Feeling When It Has Not Been Induced

Situations in which the curative feeling is completely different from the induction are often the hardest to work with because the analyst does not immediately feel the emotional communication that the patient needs. Where does the analyst find the needed feelings? The objective countertransference cannot be counted upon to provide all the feelings the patient may need to experience from the analyst. Some patients do (eventually!) manage to induce all the feelings that they need to experience in order to loosen their repetitions, but this is rare. In order to provide the "different enough to be curative" dimension of curative emotional experience, the analyst must often summon the needed feelings within himself through a process of auto-induction. The analyst may have to actively and deliberately place himself in the position of an ideal parent to the child. Because the needed intervention will be completely different from the objective countertransference, it may feel inauthentic, and it may take years to find.

For example, after several sessions one analyst had an intensely negative countertransference to a patient. At first she was interested in the patient because he was involved in a profession that intrigued her and was referred by another patient whom she very much enjoyed. But she was soon disappointed in him. She found him intensely irritating. The patient was profoundly depressed, yet superficially agreeable. The analyst felt he was obsequious, and she hated him with a disdain that was far outside her usual range of feeling.

The induction was clearly objective. Numerous employers had rejected the patient, and, over time, all of his friends had abandoned him. The analyst hypothesized that the patient had developed a superficial false-self to cover the memory of two parents who both loathed him and to avoid being loathed in the present. But try as he might, he was unable to escape the repetition. The analyst had a strong sense that the patient needed a loving communication, but didn't feel she could provide it. During the first couple of years, the most loving thing she could do was to contain her loathing, while forcing herself to treat him nicely—but not overly so. She reminded herself that the parents hated the patient and tried to imagine loving the patient as a baby. Although this felt inauthentic, she noticed small changes in the treatment that suggested this approach would work. After two years, during which time the analyst was nearly silent and struggling with her feelings, the patient occasionally reported feeling better, and the analyst occasionally felt that she enjoyed him. Slowly, these two feelings amplified each other as the analyst began to have loving feelings that felt more genuine.

In this case, the curative feeling differed in every way from the objective countertransference. The analyst was able to make communications that were sufficiently different only after she had intellectually determined what the patient needed. However, it was, in a sense, the opposite of the countertransference, and in that way, the countertransference guided the analyst to it.

Such situations are obviously the hardest to manage and require the most imagination and capacity for emotional self-control. The patient who has pitilessly demeaned the analyst for years may need the analyst to empathize with his inability to feel understood by the analyst. Or the patient whom the analyst cherishes and adores may need the analyst to sometimes reject or disapprove of him. It may take a long time for the analyst to realize this, and even longer before he can have the feeling with sufficient intensity to communicate it to the patient. Nevertheless, I have found that the analyst can usually summon up the feeling, provided he can overcome his own resistances to experiencing and communicating it.

When the patient needs the feeling that he induces in the analyst, and the analyst uses the feeling, the progress of the analysis feels smooth, natural, and spontaneous. But when the patient needs a feeling that he does not induce in the analyst, the analysis can feel stalemated. But this may not, in fact, be the case. The apparent lack of progress may mean that the patient isn't ready to experience the needed feeling. What is more, the struggle to find the needed feeling can be valuable because the patient often knows, on some level, that the analyst has struggled to give him what he emotionally needs. But not every patient will feel this way. Some may have been ready for the feeling earlier and may just feel frustrated that the analyst took such a long time to come around to it. It would be ideal if we had some way of consistently referring patients to the analysts who will have the right feelings for them. Absent such a plan, there is nothing to be done about the problem. The analyst can't communicate a feeling that he doesn't have (Freud, 1937). At some point, both the patient and the analyst must come to terms with the analyst's limitations in this area.

On a more positive note, I am consistently surprised by how frequently so many analysts, each with the limitations imposed by their own subjectivity, are able to find the needed feelings so often, for so many of their patients.

Summary: Finding the Curative Emotional Communication

There is, unfortunately, no formula for finding the curative emotional communication. No amount of information or understanding of the patient can provide the answer with certainty, and every analyst will encounter idiosyncratic cases in which he seems to stumble on the right feeling by accident. Nevertheless, the various ways that the curative emotional communication can be related to the countertransference defines the range of the most likely possibilities. In the vast majority of the cases, the curative expressive intervention will be related, in some way, to either the induction or the content of the session. So, the list of ways that the intervention can be related to the induction, can serve as a sort of decision tree that allows one to consider the various possibilities in an organized fashion. With this in mind, the analyst should:

First: Consider whether the objective countertransference itself— either as he experiences it or with its intensity modified in some way— is the curative emotional communication. In this case, the analyst communicates the same specific feeling that he experiences. This is the easiest situation to work with.

Next: Consider whether the countertransference requires a significant change in intensity. In this situation, the analyst, again, has the right feeling, but the intensity is either too high or too low. If too high, it tends to disrupt the patient; if not intense enough, the emotional communication may not have any impact on the patient. Changing the intensity of the emotional communication requires a degree of emotional imagination by the analyst, but this is not usually difficult to achieve.

Then: Consider whether the analyst is feeling approximately the specific feeling, but in the wrong mode of relatedness; that is, the emotional communication may have to be made in a different mode of relatedness than was felt by the analyst. In this case, the analyst should attempt to feel the same feeling he already has, but in a different mode of relatedness. For example, if he believes he feels the fear in the object mode, he should attempt to experience it as the patient's fear. Usually, the patient's history will show a pattern of feeling consistently misunderstood within many relationships in which he usually receives the feeling opposite to the one he expects and wants.

Cases in which the analyst must change the mode of relatedness of the feeling require more mental effort on the part of the analyst, but they are often accompanied by a moment of sudden recognition. Once the feeling is experienced in a different mode of relatedness, the clinical encounter is completely changed but often makes more sense.

Finally: Consider whether the patient needs an emotional communication that is completely different from the countertransference in both specific feeling and mode of relatedness. Even if the countertransference is objectively induced, the analyst must consider what the patient needs in order not to have a repetition of his usual experience. The analyst may need to intellectually determine what the patient needs and then summon the feeling within himself through a process of autoinduction. These cases are usually the most difficult to manage, and they do require the most creativity and therapeutic skill. But with time, and a commitment to the patient, the right feeling can usually be found.

REFERENCES

Alexander, F. (1925), A metaphysical description of the process of cure. *International Journal of Psychoanalysis,* 6:13–34.

Balint, M. (1952), *Primary Love and Psycho-Analytic Technique.* London: Hogarth.

Balint, M. (1968), *The Basic Fault.* London: Tavistock Publications.

Bernstein, A. (1992), Beyond countertransference: the love that cures. *Modern Psychoanalysis,* 17:15–31.

Bernstein, J. (1981), An approach to the management of treatment impasses. *Modern Psychoanalysis,* 6:201–220.

Bernstein, J. (1993), Using the countertransference resistance. *Modern Psychoanalysis,* 18:71–80.

Ernsberger, C. (1979), The concept of countertransference as therapeutic instrument: its early history. *Modern Psychoanalysis,* 4:141–164.

Ernsberger, C. (1990), Modern countertransference theory: some elaborations and clinical illustrations. *Modern Psychoanalysis,* 15:11–31.

Ferenczi, S. (1955), *Final Contributions to the Problems and Methods of Psycho-analysis.* London: Hogarth Press.

Freud, S. (1937), Analysis terminable and interminable. *Standard Edition.* London: Hogarth Press, 23:209–253.

Hayden, S. (1983), The toxic response in modern psychoanalysis. *Modern Psychoanalysis,* 8:3–16.

Kirman, J. (1983), Modern psychoanalysis and intimacy: treatment of the narcissistic personality. *Modern Psychoanalysis,* 8:17–34.

Kirman, J. (1998), One-person or two-person psychology. *Modern Psychoanalysis,* 23:3–22.

Kirman, W. (1980a), Countertransference in facilitating intimacy and communication. *Modern Psychoanalysis,* 5:131–145.

Kirman, W. (1980b), Citation from course in maturational process, Center for Modern Psychoanalytic Studies, New York, NY. Fall, 1980.

Laquercia, T. (1992), The anaclitic environment: the emerging challenge for the analyst. *Modern Psychoanalysis,* 17:35–42.

Laquercia, T. (1998), Symbolic imagery: an aspect of unverbalized communication. *Modern Psychoanalysis,* 20:23–33.

Liegner, E. (1980), The hate that cures: the psychological reversibility of schizophrenia. *Modern Psychoanalysis,* 5:5–95.

Liegner, E. (1991), The anaclitic countertransference. *Modern Psychoanalysis,* 16:5–13.

Liegner, E. (1995), The anaclitic countertransference in resistance resolution. *Modern Psychoanalysis,* 20:153–164.

Margolis, B. (1978), Narcissistic countertransference: emotional availability and case management. *Modern Psychoanalysis,* 3:161–177.

Margolis, B. (1979), Narcissistic transference: the product of overlapping self and object fields. *Modern Psychoanalysis,* 4:131–140.

Margolis, B. (1994), Narcissistic transference: further considerations. *Modern Psychoanalysis,* 19:149–159.

Marshall, R. (1993), Comparisons, contrasts, and convergences. *Modern Psychoanalysis,* 16:25–34.

Meadow, P. W. (1987), The myth of the impersonal analyst. *Modern Psychoanalysis,* 12:131–150.

Meadow, P. W. (1988), Emotional education: the theory and process of training psychoanalysts. *Modern Psychoanalysis,* 13:211–388.

Meadow, P. W. (1989), How we aim to be with patients. *Modern Psychoanalysis,* 14:145–162.

Meadow, P. W. (1991), Resonating with the psychotic patient. *Modern Psychoanalysis.* 16:87–103.

Moreau Ricaud, M. (2000), *Michael Balint: Le Renouveau de L'école de Budapest.* Toulouse, France: Érès.

Sechehaye, M. (1951), *Symbolic Realization: A New Method of Psychotherapy Applied to a Case of Schizophrenia.* New York: International Universities Press.

Sherman, M. (1983), Emotional communication in modern psychoanalysis: some Freudian origins and comparisons. *Modern Psychoanalysis,* 8:173–189.

Spotnitz, H. (1976), *Psychotherapy of Preoedipal Conditions: Schizophrenia and Severe Character Disorders.* New York: Jason Aronson.

Spotnitz, H. (1983), Countertransference with the psychotic patient: value of the positive anaclitic countertransference. *Modern Psychoanalysis,* 8:169–172.

Spotnitz, H. (1989), Therapeutic countertransference: interventions with the schizophrenic patient. *Modern Psychoanalysis,* 14:3–20.

Spotnitz, H. (2004), *Modern Psychoanalysis of the Schizophrenic Patient.* 2nd ed. New York: YBK Publishers.

Weinstein, R. S. (1986), Should analysts love their patients? *Modern Psychoanalysis,* 11:103–110.

Winnnicott, D. W. (1949), Hate in the countertransference. *International Journal of Psychoanalysis,* 30:69–74.

24 East 12th Street, #505
New York, NY 10003
pgeltner@earthlink.net

Modern Psychoanalysis
Vol. XXXII, No. 1, 2007

Fear of the Empty Self: The Motivations for Genital Exhibitionism

LISA PIEMONT

Three case studies demonstrate the character dynamics and psychological motivations common to genital exhibitionists. Fears of psychic emptiness and powerlessness, abuse, and neglect in the early maternal environment and the attachment of libidinal drives to external objects appear as motivational factors for this disorder. The author explores the efficacy of individual and group treatment methods with recommendations for best practices in both modalities.

McDougall (1995) introduced the concept of neosexualities in *The Many Faces of Eros: A Psychoanalytic Exploration of Human Sexuality*. In this groundbreaking work, she explained that perverse sexual expressions are a unique attempt to alleviate tensions surrounding early psychic anxieties. Exhibitionism is a specific adaptive expression of this human tendency. Perhaps because exhibitionism is a "non-contact" crime, the psychological impact on women and children can be minimized—but it is a threatening act suggesting that the perpetrator intends a progression of his sexually aggressive behavior and indicating a dangerous incapacity to control impulses. The need for effective treatment of this condition is clear since arrest and conviction rarely diminishes the offender's desire to perform the acts again once released (Stoller, 1975).

Three composite portraits, presented here as case examples, describe common patterns of deviant sexual behavior beginning in adolescence

© 2007 CMPS/*Modern Psychoanalysis*, Vol. 32, No. 1

and reports of such behavior during decades of treatment. Discussion of the motivational factors commonly found in cases of exhibitionism follows the case examples. The discussion includes an exploration of transference and countertransference issues that may arise during a course of treatment, references to relevant literature and theoretical considerations, and recommendations for treatment approaches in assisting individuals who display this behavior.

Composite Case Examples

The following "case examples" are actually composite portraits based on several real patients. Because they rely on a significant degree of similarity to be seen in the histories and behaviors of many such patients, I believe they accurately, to a meaningful degree, represent issues that patients and therapists confront in such cases and in such lives.

In general, men who exhibit themselves present for treatment with a great deal of psychic distress about their impulses, over which they feel they have no control. They suffer greatly about their behavior and experience just as much ego-dissonance as they experience id-satisfaction about their histories of acting out. Yet, the compulsion to engage in the behavior overrides their strong concerns about consequences as well as the shame and guilt they associate with these acts.

Case Vignette 1

Mr. K goes to the park on his lunch hour and finds a shady grove. He unzips his pants, exposes himself, and begins to masturbate. Soon, a group of women walk nearby, but instead of hiding himself from them, he moves forward. He wants them to see his genitals so he can experience their reaction. In this exact moment he is gratified. The women's expressions of shock, disgust, and fear provoke the greatest sexual excitement he can experience. Later in the day, however, he is ashamed of himself and disgusted by his behavior. He vows not to do it again. He succeeds for three or four days in avoiding the park at lunch but eventually returns to repeat the scenario time and again.

When Mr. K presents for individual treatment in an outpatient setting, he reports that he has engaged in exhibitionism for over 20 years and describes a childhood history of unrelenting verbal and emotional abuse by his mother. He feels unable to stop his sexual behavior and is very concerned about getting caught. He holds a position of importance in an academic institution and is certain he will lose his job if criminal charges are ever filed against him. He also reports a history of instability in his romantic relationships: he has been divorced twice and is currently engaged to be married again.

In his initial sessions, Mr. K states that he wants to stop exhibiting himself. He blames his exhibitionism on stress and identifies work and intimate relationships as the particular areas to be addressed. Initially, he devotes his sessions to managing the specific stressful issues in work and personal relationships. At work, he has an intense need for approval and feels easily slighted. He has a great deal of difficulty coping with negative reactions from others or with any perceived criticism. He also struggles with feeling unacknowledged, and feels angry that he works harder and longer than his colleagues, with insufficient reward or recognition. When he does receive praise, his pleasure in it is short-lived as if the experience cannot be retained for prolonged or future gratification. When he is not regularly acknowledged by peers and superiors, he tends to lose interest in performing his work duties; boredom and inertia set in. This is the mental context in which his deviant fantasies emerge as he begins to plan his next episode of acting out.

His relationships with females disappoint him. He often feels rejected when his emotional needs are not met. He tends to express his disappointment in an abusive manner, and his relationships end when the women decide they feel too criticized and hopeless about satisfying him. Like his work, romantic relationships have fallen short of satisfying his need for emotional stimulation. A contemptuous boredom with his romantic partner develops, and it is in this state that he begins to plan his next act of exhibitionism. At the time he begins treatment, he is hoping to train his new fiancée so that she will understand his needs fully and be able to respond to him better than his previous partners.

After four years of weekly sessions, during which he presents as free of compulsive exhibitionism, as well as periodic couples sessions when his relationship begins to deteriorate, Mr. K admits to me that he has never given up his exhibitionism. He has been acting out throughout the time we have worked together, and during his most recent episode his victim instantly called the police on her cell phone. He is terrified of being caught and seems to be devastated by the experience of revealing his secret to me once again. There is a strong emotional charge to his disclosure, and although he expresses shame and remorse, he also seems excited as he reveals the truth. I wonder about the paradox—the patient has been keeping a secret from me (not being known) while simultaneously exposing himself elsewhere (being excessively known). Is he aroused in some way by the power of deceiving me? I am caught off guard when he reveals the truth to me—shocked at my own naïveté and his deceitfulness.

Nothing in four years of treatment with Mr. K suggested that he was continuing his sexual acting out. In retrospect, though, it seems evident that he was completely detached from his sexual motivations and behaviors, as was I, as if a great thick wall existed between us that neither one of us mentioned. I recognize that in the countertransference with Mr. K, I often experience a great emptiness within him and a wish to fill that void, perhaps because it frightens me. I remember feeling that in this patient's emptiness are hidden forms of primitive rage that he has repressed.

In group treatment for sexual offenders modeled after twelve-step programs, the phrase "Secrets keep you sick" is repeated as a warning that, unless the offender openly reports all his fantasies and behaviors, the memory of them will fester and intensify, only to grab hold of him when he is least suspecting that he remains interested in the sexual deviance. Offenders who wish to discontinue their deviant sexual behavior are encouraged to share their secret fantasies and behaviors with their peers and therapist in order to diminish the intensity of the arousal they have associated with the acts and fantasies. Because the group members and therapist do not respond with shock and fear, the offender does not experience sexual gratification in sharing his fantasies in the group. Over time he becomes desensitized to the material.

In individual treatment, the rules of analysis provide the structure within which the dynamics of the patient's sexual deviance can be manifested and explored. The rules of lying on the couch, the suggestion to speak on the five subjects (Spotnitz, 2004) in every session, the structure provided by arriving on time and paying on time—all these elicit various resistances that offer the therapist and the patient an opportunity to understand how and why the sexual-offense dynamic persists. In my work with Mr. K, I do not initially make the suggestion that he speak on each of the five subjects in every session. Instead, I follow the contact function (Margolis, 1994a) and allow long silences whenever they occur. Possibly, his continued exhibitionism could have been curtailed by the requirement to discuss his sexual deviance in every session and by analysis of his resistance to doing so.

Case Vignette 2

Mr. B reports that he began exposing himself when he was 14. He was ill much of the time and home from school. He recalls that he was painfully bored and lonely. Every day he watched as the schools let out, standing in his bedroom window exposing himself to the girls as they passed by. Now 54 years old and unemployed, he drives around town after school hours and lures girls to his car window where he shows them his exposed penis. At the moment he catches their attention, he is thrilled and aroused by their fearful and disgusted response. Later, he feels ashamed and afraid of being turned in to the police. He repeats this scenario on a daily basis. Mr. B presents for group treatment in a prison setting. He is silent for the first several weeks of meetings. When invited to speak, he comments sarcastically and caustically about what another group member has shared. He laughs and enjoys the sexual material described by his peers. Several group members object aggressively to his apparent pleasure-seeking approach to group sessions. He modifies his responses and adopts a disingenuous affinity for moralizing and reprimanding. A group member comments, "First you're like the bad boy who's here to snicker and have fun. Now you're like the parish priest or the therapist assistant. Who are you, anyway?" After this confrontation, Mr. B withdraws for several weeks. When he is asked why he no longer participates, he comments that he finds the group boring. Group members react to this angrily, suggesting that he take more responsibility for his group experience by finding a way to participate constructively.

Group members struggle to understand Mr. B and elicit meaningful dialogue from him about his experience. He wishes to remain unknown to the group: unable to say who he is, unable to form a therapeutic attachment to the group members. At the same time, he gains the group members' frustrated attention. Finally, after many sessions in which the group attempts to "get answers" from Mr. B, a member asks, "Are we really going to spend another session giving him all the attention? What's the point? Until he figures out who he is, we never will, and we're just wasting our time while he soaks it all in and stops everyone else from getting the help they need."

The dynamics of Mr. B's exhibitionism are manifested in his transference to the group. His manner of contacting the group prevents understanding and provides him with an emotional arousal as he controls others by drawing them close, only to frustrate and withhold. Over time the group attempts to work with him on this dynamic when it occurs, and he is able to participate in the process more fully. First, group members share with him their experience that he seems to want to be the center of attention, but that his demeanor ensures that their responses to him will be negative. Later, the group encourages him to seek attention in a socially appropriate manner, by asking for emotional attention when he wants it and specifying to the group exactly what kind of response would be therapeutic. It is important to note that his approach to treatment changes *only* after he is confronted in the group for this symbolic sexual offending: for seeking sexual stimulation in group members' material, for tending to frustrate and attack, and for withholding in order to control. His preference for gratifying himself by provoking the group into an angry state diminishes as he learns to engage productively by asking directly for emotional feeding from the group members and the therapist. He also begins to describe his life experience to the group for the first time: he tells the group that his father left his mother when he was born, and he always felt he was a burden to her. He describes longstanding feelings of neglect and a certainty that he was not wanted.

Joseph (1971) describes the way in which an exhibitionist's hidden deviance manifests in treatment relationships. She presents the case of a male patient whose analysis illustrates how the dynamics of sexual perversion can be represented in the transference and countertransference material. Joseph's patient suffered from dissatisfaction in interpersonal relationships because of his intense interest in sadistic and masochistic sexual practices. While Joseph analyzed his sadism, his sessions were characterized by silence and passivity:

> Usually, after what might be seen by myself as a helpful interpretation, he would go into a very heavy silence, often with deep breathing, then frequently he would slowly emerge from it, making rather trite wordy remarks, so that the whole feeling was flat and verbose; or the silence would go on as if I had to make the next move. . . . It was clear that in this way, my work was kept sterile. (pp. 444–445)

Mr. B, like Joseph's patient, nullifies the group process when he uses group interactions for indirect satisfaction of his libidinal fantasies. Interpreting her patient's silent inductions, Joseph explains:

> I could show him in some detail his actual passivity as an attempt to stimulate me, so as to project into me feelings not only of excitement but that I should want to rouse him into activity, beat him, or be cruel to him. (pp. 445–446)

Like Mr. B's use of the group to stimulate and excite himself, Joseph's patient used the communication process—the giving and receiving of words—to stimulate, excite, and sexualize the analysis, thereby destroying its strength, not openly through aggression or hostility but covertly through the giving and withholding of words. Mr. B uses titillation, sarcasm, and moralizing to destroy the treatment process in the group and secure the primitive defenses against knowing himself.

Case Vignette 3

Mr. L reports that he was humiliated and sexually harassed at a boys' summer camp when he was 12. He tried to complain to the camp director, but his complaints fell on deaf ears. After he returned to school in the fall, the boys who knew him at camp continued to tease and taunt him about the abuse he experienced there. He was horrified when his female schoolmates observed the teasing and was filled with rage and feelings of powerlessness. He discovered some pornography in his father's desk at home and absorbed himself in excited fantasies of sexual acceptance from the women in the magazines. Over time, he became preoccupied with the need for sexual approval and admiration, finding himself at age 27 walking down crowded streets with his pants open and his penis exposed. He reports that he hoped for a positive response from an unsuspecting female passerby, but he was aroused instead by her shocked horror when she observed his behavior.

Mr. L seeks treatment on the advice of his attorney, while he awaits trial on a sexual assault charge. He has exposed himself to a woman in an elevator. According to her statement, he threatened to assault her when he exposed his penis. He asked if she likes this kind of thing. Mr. L presents as superficially concerned about the charges against him and sincerely uncomprehending of the severity of his victim's reaction. He claims that all she had to do was say no, and he seems to have no sense of what terrified her. He is defensive and attempts to explain to me that he meant no harm. He laughs contemptuously when he describes his view of the police ineptitude during the investigation of his behavior and seems to have a need to place himself above it all. His biggest mistake in the matter, as he identifies it, was doing it in an elevator. He also feels that he chose the wrong person. He "guessed her wrong." She seemed like "a sexual type" but turned out not to be.

As Mr. L's legal problems unfold, he continues to attend therapy and presents a strong resistance to being helped with his compulsion. Unlike Mr. K, who hid his continued exhibitionism from me, he discusses the sexual offense in every session. Yet he does so in a way that appears to reinforce the very cognitive processes and defensive operations supporting the behavior: he minimizes ("They usually don't see me"), rationalizes ("I don't have a girlfriend right now"), and blames stress and fatigue for his behavior. Mr. L is equally contemptuous regarding the treatment. He says it is useless and boring, and he resents the pressure to attend. I am annoyed. I use my negative feelings to join his resistant and negative attitudes: "We are stuck with each other," I say. "Why does your lawyer insist on this charade?" And sometimes I add, "I agree, this is a boring session."

Finally, Mr. L's fear of a possible prison term and his belief that jail represents the threat of "disappearing forever" motivate a change in his approach to the sessions. He begins to express his fear of disappearing. When asked to explore or explain this fear, he becomes highly anxious and bothered by the realization that he does not know what the fear is about or why it is on his mind so persistently. He begins to ask for help hesitantly because he is reluctant to experience not knowing something about himself. As he becomes more emotionally open in sessions, it emerges that he is, in fact, terrified of not knowing himself. He says he often feels "like an empty void" or "an empty shell," and he remains deeply perplexed about the bizarre nature of his exhibitionism.

He begins to reveal powerfully violent sexual fantasies and a tendency to spend a great deal of time with internet pornography. In addition to his exhibitionism, he describes a long-standing addiction to pornography that started in early adolescence. When he describes his father's aggressive personality and his mother's passivity, he remembers how his father demeaned his mother by calling her fat and ugly. His escape into pornography helped him to identify with his father and sublimate his rage toward his mother for her helplessness. As he begins to speak about his childhood sexual abuse at summer camp, a more genuine emotional attachment to the therapist and the treatment emerge.

Mr. L's fear of disappearing entirely by going to prison motivates him to seek help in the treatment and to allow himself to be known and seen authentically for the first time since his childhood abuse. At this point, something new emerges in the countertransference: nurturing and loving feelings are experienced, and it is possible to provide Mr. L with an appropriately accepting emotional environment in which he can mature sufficiently to overcome his compulsions.

Shepherd (2001) explains:

[T]he negative narcissistic transference is necessary as long as the patient needs it, but it is not necessary longer than the patient needs it. A moment comes when the patient begins to be able to indicate his readiness for something else, something new. This is the anaclitic moment within the negative narcissistic state. (p. 80)

When Mr. L presented for treatment in a highly negative state, he was predisposed to protect himself from real contact with the world, and to resist emerging from his narcissism by attacking the value of everything around him and placing blame for his problems outside of himself. This did not change until the "anaclitic moment" occurred in the countertransference. Only then were the patient and the therapist ready to experience an exchange of small doses of the positive affect states that serve as the building blocks of a more mature ego.

Discussion

The men described in the case vignettes above experienced very early anxieties about psychic emptiness, which originated in traumatic childhood experiences of abuse or neglect in the maternal environment. These patients present material in their treatment that shows evidence of inadequate or damaged maternal introjects, resulting in an impaired capacity for mirroring and being mirrored. They expel feelings of powerlessness through projective identification during acts of exhibitionism when they need to master the overwhelming anxieties surrounding emptiness. Often this emptiness is experienced as or labeled "boredom."

Describing the etiology of deviant sexuality, McDougall (1995) says:

> In attempting to conceptualize the internalizations that take place between mother and infant, the terms *incorporation* and *introjection* are more appropriate than *identification*. At this stage of development, the mother's unconscious fears and wishes play a predominant role in the early structural development of the psyche. (p.180)

Patients who display their genitals are replicating early processes first experienced with a mother who might have transmitted to her children "a body-image that is fragile, alienated, devoid of eroticism or even mutilated." Since the soma is indistinguishable from the early psyche in terms of the development of the self, we can extrapolate that it is also the psyche that is established as fragile, alienated, devoid of eroticism, and mutilated. This "lack of a stable introjective constellation" (p.183) gives rise to intense states of psychic anxiety surrounding fears of emptiness, void, or disintegration of the fragile self (p.180).

Stoller (1975) also described the compulsive sexual behavior of exhibitionists as a defense against boredom. If boredom refers to a state of understimulation that threatens these structurally fragile and alienated patients with a form of psychic emptiness, the cases described herein support Stoller's theory. He named "risk, revenge, and triumph" as motivating factors for the exhibitionist's sexual scenarios (p.128). Both Mr. K and Mr. B described boredom as precipitating mood states that occurred prior to their acts of exhibitionism, and Mr. L, who complained that the treatment was boring, repeated his fear of "disappearing forever" if his behavior led to a prison term. Case histories of exhibitionists typically include scenarios with over- or understimulating maternal objects. Under these conditions, an infant cannot incorporate positive maternal imagos in the service of the developing self. The sense of void, of psychic death, is real to both patient and therapist. The early introjects are the building blocks of the developing ego. Without the necessary experiences, there is a real sense of void. Action defenses are produced in response to the early anxieties described by McDougall (1995) and have their basis in deficits resulting from interactions with a psychically incomplete maternal object. Acting out creates internal stimulation that distracts the exhibitionist from emptiness that borders on psychic disintegration and binds the fragile psyche by directing the aggressive drive outward onto objects in the environment.

As a result of the early deficits and the consequent void in the earliest areas of psychic development, the patient's capacity for mirroring and being mirrored is impaired. The experience of the early mother as mirror did not occur, so it is impossible to give and receive emotionally on an interpersonal basis in adulthood. This deficit can be observed in the social lives of some exhibitionists. Their awareness of how they are perceived by others is limited. They over- or underestimate how they are regarded by their contemporaries and superiors. These deficits suggest trauma and arrest during the oral stage when objects are taken in and pushed out through the mouth for physical nourishment and through the eyes for emotional nourishment. Margolis (1994b) describes the psychological need for mirroring that is evident in patients who suffer from narcissistic conditions. Like McDougall, Margolis suggests that such patients have introjected damaging aspects of the early mothering environment. As an infant, the patient internalized an image of a frustrating maternal object and became identified with it. He therefore turned away from perceiving the world as a source of true emotional nourishment, invoking the narcissistic defense and negation as primary methods for establishing psychic equilibrium.

When these patients appear for treatment, they are typically entrenched in highly negative emotional and cognitive states. During the initial phase of treatment when the negative narcissistic transference is established, the therapist reflects back to the patient negative impressions of himself and the world (Margolis, 1994b). Shepherd (2001) elaborates:

> For a long period of time, analyst and patient engage in some version of repeated verbalization of negative impressions. The situation seems endless. Feelings of hopelessness are paramount. They are frozen together in an eternal negative symbiosis.
>
> What is the way out? Little by little, as the patient talks and pieces together fragmented images and affects, making more mind, as his defenses are supported and as some of the destructive aggression is bound, a very subtle change occurs. He begins to be able to hint at what he needs. (pp. 80–81)

In patients who suffer from sexual perversions, negative transference states are highly common. At first, it may seem that their negativity is in response to having been discovered and ordered for treatment or is a resistance to cooperating with a perceived authority. But their negative disposition originated in the early maternal environment and the narcissistic defense that developed in the face of maternal neglect or abuse.

Indeed, Stoller (1975) theorized that sexual perversion is based in feelings of primitive hate that an infant experiences in his early environment. He thought that the exhibitionist is engaged in an act of undoing an early traumatic experience of powerlessness: by frightening a victim, the exhibitionist is experiencing his own fears and humiliations, externalized in the form of his victim's response to his behavior. Stoller states:

> [T]he woman who is shocked, who becomes angry and, best of all, frightened, who creates a fuss, and who brings on the police proves that he has reversed the childhood situation. She is complying with a necessary part of his perversion; now she is the attacked one and he the attacker. (p. 131)

Resistances to feelings of powerlessness are strong motivators for exhibitionistic behavior. Acting out the behavior is a method for remaining out of contact with the emotional motivation; action defenses make it possible to frame the motivation as purely sexual or as a response to stress, such as "too much work" or "not enough money." The actions serve to provide stimulation, which prevents awareness of the psychic void. The deficits in the exhibitionist's processes related to early mirroring and the reservoirs of unconscious primitive hate typically manifest in seeking negative affect states in his victims. Patients who suffer from exhibitionism describe arousal to specific kinds of reactions in their victims. Whereas they may consciously fantasize about a woman responding with sexual interest to their exposure, they are ultimately most aroused by the shock and fear they elicit. The extreme state of excitement that is evoked by their victim's fear serves as a defense against states of emptiness experienced as boredom. Patients often describe disappointment when victims do not provide the exciting response of shock and fear. One offender explained his devastation when a group of high school girls reacted to his exposure by laughing and taunting him. He became briefly suicidal after this particular episode but soon sought a corrective experience in which he did acquire a fearful response from his next victim.

In addition to its role as a defense against the psychic emptiness experienced as "boredom," exhibitionism has an addictive component. McDougall (1995) observed that in the addictive aspects of some sexual perversions

> There is a *final defiance of death itself,* which takes two forms. First, there is an omnipotent stance ("Nothing can touch me—death is for the others"). Then, when this grandiose form of defense breaks down and the sense of inner deadness can no longer be denied, there is a yielding to the death impulses. (pp.188–189)

The deadness, or void, represents a kind of psychic annihilation that is both feared and wanted.

In addiction, emotional relations remain tied to external objects who are not attached to established introjects. The exhibitionist seeks the loving and admiring eyes of the mother but does not have an internal representation of her as the loving, approving caregiver. His exhibitionism must be repeated again and again because the emotional experience is attached to an external source. There is a conflict, however. The exhibitionist's behavior is designed to elicit a negative reaction. The experience of looking and being looked at with an early maternal object was traumatic in some way: insufficient, overstimulating, hostile, abandoning, disturbing. The exhibitionist is motivated to replicate this hostile early interaction in order to master the trauma of the original intense disturbance. He both wants and fears this psychic death. He unconsciously fantasizes tension discharge that would result in becoming completely empty (free of tension) but also psychically dead.

In the course of treating this condition, the dynamics of early trauma that motivate the behavior emerge in the transference and countertransference material. Whereas the patient strongly wishes to keep the deviant sexual dynamic hidden, it is enacted in the treatment. For Mr. K, it appeared in the form of distressing surprises—he kept his ongoing exhibitionism secret for many years; Mr. B used the group to express his need for sexualized control-seeking by evoking their negative reactions and putting himself at the center of the group's negative attention; and Mr. L externalized the narcissistic defense by expressing contempt toward authority figures and minimizing his problems. Later, his fears of disappearing and of powerlessness became conscious and were expressed openly.

In order for the enactment to be relinquished, it must cease to feel rewarding, either by desensitization to the stimuli over time or by the negative kind of exposure Mr. B experienced in his group (which extinguished the arousal he experienced in keeping his fantasies a secret). While the therapist works to assist the patient in relinquishing the more primitive defenses, it is helpful to support and encourage the development of more mature defenses that are consistent with the exhibitionistic character. The therapist can help the patient to sublimate the need for approval, acceptance, and admiration into adaptive creative activities.

In the cases of Mr. B and Mr. L the therapist addressed the exhibitionists' arousal by his victims' fear and the possible addiction to stimulation-seeking behavior by supporting a progressive learned tolerance for undesired affect states, such as loneliness and boredom. Patients were helped in group and individual sessions to explore those feelings and their fears about experiencing them. They also were helped to experience that the therapist and group members were able to have and hold those difficult feelings without being annihilated by them. In this process, evidence of early maternal over- and under-stimulation emerged. The patients learned to guide the group members and the therapist in providing the appropriate level of stimulation so that they could remain in contact with the process during sessions. Mr. B learned to say when he wanted some special attention or was feeling neglected. Mr. L talked in his individual sessions about feeling bored and was able to describe his fears of annihilation related to boredom.

Group work with sexual offenders is a common mode of treatment (Salter, 1988). Group members model disclosure of their behaviors and fantasies, patients easily form narcissistic transferences to other group members, and the therapist can use herself to support or to challenge resistances in individuals and the group as a whole. In a group that was held in a prison setting, members became adept at identifying perverse transferences to the group when these were displayed by individual group members. There was group vigilance about this phenomenon, but a group resistance to open exploration of deviant sexuality evolved. Group members kept asking each other if the disclosures were too stimulating and causing sexual arousal. The wish to feel aroused by the material was expressed as a fear, and the group sought prohibitions. The therapist became concerned that the process might shut down entirely and asked if the group members could allow enough verbal acting out in the group to enable the sharing of material. The group agreed upon a "save your comments until the end" approach. Direct challenges from group members, when delivered in tolerable doses, progressively diminished the perpetrator's arousal of their sexual actions and fantasies.

Individual treatment with exhibitionists is more difficult than group work. The bilateral process of confrontation and support is not available as it is in a group modality. The individual therapist is advised to ask herself and her supervisor from the onset where the exhibitionism is manifesting in the patient's life in and outside the sessions. In individual treatment in an outpatient setting, the rules of treatment can be invoked to provide structure and opportunity for resolving treatment resistances that might appear in the transference. The therapist responded to Mr. K by simply following direct contacts during sessions with joining responses, with the result that important material related to his offense behaviors was omitted while he continued to act out in the community. As I mentioned, there was a feeling of great distance in the treatment relationship, and anaclitic feelings did not emerge while he kept his behavior a secret. Mr. L, also treated on an individual basis, spoke readily on a range of topics, entered into a negative narcissistic union (Meadow, 1992), and slowly, from the safety of the narcissistic transference, became aware of his dependency needs and fears of non-existence.

Patients can be helped to discover more socially acceptable forms of exhibitionism. For example, one patient discovered an enjoyment of singing at a karaoke bar, where he developed some social relationships and worked to overcome interpersonal reticence and shyness. The anticipation and excitement that developed around this new activity appeared to draw him away from pursuing his sexual behaviors as an expression of his wish to be seen. Another patient joined the group Toast Masters, where members practice giving speeches and leading seminars. This appeared to partially satisfy his need to be admired and in control.

Summary and Conclusions

The compulsion to sexually expose oneself appears to be commonly motivated by fears of psychic emptiness and interpersonal powerlessness. The absence of stable and positive maternal introjects, the need to discharge unbound infantile hatred, and the attachment of libidinal drives to external objects are common structural deficits found in persons who commit exhibitionism. Unconscious wishes to be seen, to have an effect, and to experience evidence of one's own existence through the reactions of an external object are gratified in the commission of this perverse act. Early sexual and emotional trauma often appear in the historical accounts of exhibitionists and in the transference and countertransference material that emerges during treatment. Over- and understimulating maternal environments, sexual and emotional shaming as a form of psychological abandonment, and conditioned states of hyperarousal as a defense against fears of emptiness seem to be common psychic conflicts that emerge in the treatment of exhibitionism.

The literature on perversions supports the idea that successful treatment of this condition requires the resolution of the resistance to experiencing distressing emotional and psychological states as well as the progressive building of mature introjects through the narcissistic transference to the therapist or group members.

REFERENCES

Joseph, B. (1971), A clinical contribution to the analysis of a perversion. *International Journal of Psychoanalysis*, 52: 441–449.

Margolis, B. (1994a), The contact function of the ego: its role in the therapy of the narcissistic patient. *Modern Psychoanalysis*, 19:199–210.

Margolis, B. (1994b), Joining, mirroring and psychological reflection. *Modern Psychoanalysis*, 19:211–226.

McDougall, J. (1995), *The Many Faces of Eros: A Psychoanalytic Exploration of Human Sexuality.* New York: Norton.

Meadow, P. W. (1992), The negative union. *Modern Psychoanalysis,* 17:23–33.

Salter, A. (1988), *Treating Sex Offenders and Victims: A Practical Guide.* Newbury Park, CA: SAGE Publications.

Shepherd, M. (2001), Anaclitic considerations in severe negative states. *Modern Psychoanalysis*, 26:77–85.

Spotnitz, H. (2004), *Modern Psychoanalysis of the Schizophrenic Patient: Theory and Technique,* 2nd ed. New York: YBK Publishers.

Stoller, R. J. (1975), *Perversion: The Erotic Form of Hatred.* London: Karnac Books.

95 Summit Avenue 2nd fl
Summit, NJ 07901
lpiemont@mbrac.com

Book Reviews

WORKING IN THE COUNTERTRANSFERENCE: NECESSARY ENTANGLEMENTS. Howard A. Wishnie. Lanham, MD: Rowman & Littlefield, 2005. 263 pp.

This is an engaging, useful, and easily read text that modern psychoanalysts will find generally congruent with their practice.

Wishnie begins his book with mercifully brief synopses of authors whose views are consistent with his. Among the array of frequently referenced clinicians are Kohut, Searles, Kernberg, Bollas, Epstein, Hoffman, Buie, Ogden, Winnicott, and Little. A medically trained psychoanalyst, he acknowledges the influence of major theoretical schools and infant research.

The power of Wishnie's work is in the detailed clinical cases he has selected from a practice in which he seems to have been "the therapist of last resort." His experience with drug addicts, criminals, and patients with impulse disorders is reflected in his down-to-earth and personally engaging style. The reader is led in an emotional manner through Wishnie's struggles with clinically recalcitrant and emotionally tumultuous patients. His forte is exploring with the patient the here and now without overstimulating the patient. His descriptions of his and his patients' feelings are presented in everyday, jargonless terms. He tries to stay close to his patients' experience for he believes that patients attempt to induce emotional reactions in him. Wishnie's concept of the patient's role in emotional communication is similar to Spotnitz's, and like Spotnitz, he is a master at theorizing about the patient after examining and "metabolizing" projections and countertransference reactions. He feels countertransferences are pervasive and inevitable in that patients always initiate reenactment scenarios. While not discounting the effects of projective identification, Wishnie emphasizes his search within himself for feelings similar to those of his patient. He finds that when he acts like his patients or communicates like an emotional twin, the analysis progresses.

Wishnie notes that in several instances he had inadvertently "broken the frame," for example, by ending the session ten minutes early. He finds that self-exploration and investigation with the patient about the error facilitates the analysis. The clinician is challenged to diagnose the reenactment, which is sometimes subtle and may go unnoticed by the clinician for weeks and months. The reader is likely to identify with Wishnie's travails and feel comforted that one isn't alone in not getting it right the first time.

Wishnie uses the term "harmonic resonance" to characterize the transference-countertransference interaction. He insists that the actual source of the resonance is located in the therapist's own life—stirred-up personal issues that are emotionally akin to the patient's experience. He emphasizes that the patient at some level desperately wants the therapist to experience her feelings. When the patient is convinced of this resonance (attunement, mirroring, empathic response), clinical movement occurs. Sometimes the critical moment comes about in an unplanned way. But for the most part, Wishnie spends considerable time silently analyzing the induced countertransference in order to use it to therapeutic advantage. In modern psychoanalytic terms, he spots the countertransference, determines the objective and subjective components, and formulates an intervention.

Some of Wishnie's interventions are confrontational or interpretative and seem to facilitate progressive communication. He recognizes when he misses the mark. But relying on his induced feelings, he auto-corrects and "re-joins" the patient. In meaningful detail he explains how he tries to locate the patient in his own experience, relate the reenactment to the past, and create an intervention. While he emphasizes being and experiencing with the patient, he warns of the distancing aspects in understanding the patient.

Extremely useful are his descriptions of reacting to frequent transference-countertransference resistances. For example, his handling of highly narcissistic patients who induce feelings of incompetence, invisibility, and responsibility provide the reader with the feeling, "Been there. Should have done that." He warns of "strategizing" with the patient who fascinates the therapist with the "there and then." His handling of patients who are curious about the therapist could be written by a modern psychoanalyst. Wishnie uses joining and mirroring without labeling the processes as such. In fact, he attributes movement in therapy to "mirroring with no demands." Comfortable working with hostility, he recognizes some patients' need for "a bad object."

Wishnie devotes a useful chapter to erotic transferences in which he notes that tendencies to avoid self-disclosure or to self-disclose are equally damaging. His chapter on psychopharmacology is written from the standpoint of a prescribing therapist, but it is a worthwhile read that unravels some of the countertransference tangles of referring a patient for psychiatric consultation and being an observer/participant in the co-treatment.

The reviewer had wanted to present case examples of Wishnie's work, but there are none—probably because of the complex and multi-factored process that he engages in. In a sense, this is a "how to" book that requires study, experience, and immersion. A short clinical anecdote, cited twice by Wishnie, is attributed to Margaret Little and is reminiscent of Spotnitz's threat to bash a patient's head. A frenzied patient announces that she feels compelled to smash something, perhaps Little's favorite pot. Little reacts, "I'll just about kill you if you smash that pot!" While the patient pauses, Little comments, "I think you thought that I really would kill you, or perhaps that I had done so." The patient replies, "Yes, I felt like that. It was frightful, but it was also very good. I knew you really felt something, and I so often thought you didn't feel anything at all!" (p. 58). Wishnie then analyzes Little's intervention. Although Wishnie tries to remain open to spontaneous responses triggered by patient enactments, he prefers to avoid such shoot-from-the-hip episodes.

An outstanding contribution is his in-depth discussions of how he uses induced feelings to understand interactions with the patient and then forges a plan or an intervention. Wishnie states, "When tempted to disclose something about myself in treatment, I review what I understand about the dynamic of this particular intervention and my own psychological status. Frequently, I find that I am feeling helpless, irrelevant, and excluded, or that I want to flee, or assuage a pain that seems unbearable" (p. 33). He reveals how he relies on his struggles with his own past "demons" and how his personal analyses affected his manner of working. The process by which he arrives at his intervention is worthy of study.

I recommend to all therapists Wishnie's personalized but professional account of creating ways to work in the transference and countertransference with the necessary entanglements.

Robert J. Marshall

THE SOUL, THE MIND, AND THE PSYCHOANALYST: THE CREATION OF THE PSYCHOANALYTIC SETTING IN PATIENTS WITH PSYCHOTIC ASPECTS. David Rosenfeld. London: Karnac Books, 2006. 264 pp.

A collection of detailed case studies, this book is written by an Argentinian analyst with 30 years of experience in the psychoanalytic treatment of regressed, borderline, psychotic, drug-addicted, and other severely disturbed patients. He was trained and practices in Buenos Aires, where he is a professor in the medical school of the University of Buenos Aires. His theoretical orientation and clinical style are based in the Kleinian school and demonstrate creative use of theory and technique derived not only from Freud and Klein, but also from such authors as Bion, Winnicott, Boyer, Green, Rosenfeld, Searles, and Tustin. He has lived and studied in Paris and London and served as vice-president of the International Psychoanalytical Association.

Rosenfeld is a passionate, dedicated, and exquisitely perceptive analyst. Throughout these case studies, he demonstrates what Thomas Ogden, in his foreword, describes as his extraordinary way of becoming the analyst that he intuits the patient needs at any given juncture of analysis. The great virtue of these essays is that Rosenfeld has described these various treatments in such detail that the reader can accompany him step by step in his psychoanalytic work, from the verbatim recounting of his interpretive interventions to the analysis of his own countertransference states. In this way, the book provides a revealing self-portrait of a masterful analyst at work as well as an instructive opportunity to observe the ways he uses the Kleinian framework to conceptualize his patients, formulate dynamics, and conduct the treatment. Of particular interest to modern psychoanalysts is Rosenfeld's use of transference interpretation, the rationale behind it, and the explicit language in which it is conveyed to the patient.

The patient Abelard was 18 months old when his parents were kidnapped by agents of the Pinochet military dicatorship in Chile, taken to a secret detention center, and tortured. The infant was handed over to a neighbor. He began treatment with Rosenfeld upon discharge from a psychiatric hospital, where he had been treated for a chronic psychosis. He was then 23 years old and living with his grandmother in a city quite a distance away. Rosenfeld went to see the patient at his grandmother's house. He agreed to go with him to a café because the patient didn't want his grandmother to listen to their conversation. He met with him again later that same day. The patient and his grandmother had meanwhile decided that Abelard would move to the house of an aunt who lived near Rosenfeld's office in Buenos Aires. Rosenfeld offered him a session every day and, as he says he does with similar cases, asked him to come twice a day for the first two or three months. Abelard accepted the offer.

From the outset, Rosenfeld was aware that he was treating not only the adult patient, but the child within the patient. His conceptualizations in the beginning included the idea that the patient re-creates in the transference moments of the first months of life and of his psychotic episode; that the patient encapsulates aspects of good infantile object relations in his mind as a kind of sanctuary against psychotic fragmentation, what Rosenfeld calls "autistic encapsulation"; and, lastly, that in the face of a real, severe trauma, all introjections or introjected identifications can disappear. The patient thus experiences a catastrophic loss of internal objects and emotional connection, i.e., a psychic void.

A session several months into the treatment demonstrates Rosenfeld's remarkable agility in grasping what is happening in the analytic relationship from moment to moment, shifting from direct interpretation of the transference to mirroring and joining to emotional communication—all within the space of a single hour.

> P: When I left the last session, I went to take the bus, and I told the driver, "a ticket for Belgrano." Then the driver said, "It isn't this bus, take the one that goes in the opposite direction." So I crossed the street and took the bus going the other way. And the next driver said, "No, you're wrong, it's the other way." You know, Dr Rosenfeld? The bus drivers are crazy, crazy. . . . You can't trust anybody, they drive me crazy.
> [Long silence.]

> A: Maybe you think I'm a crazy driver too, that I'm going to take you just anywhere in this treatment. Maybe you're afraid I'll drive the treatment so badly that you'll have to go back to the hospital where you were hospitalized. This must be your way to express your fear, your distrust of me. Like that crazy bus driver, you don't know whether I'm driving this treatment well or not.

> P: [laughs]: Well, the truth is, when I was in the hospital, one doctor would talk to me a little bit, another one didn't talk to me at all . . . they had me going from here to there.

> A: It's good for you to express your distrust of me.

> After a long silence the patient begins to sing and goes on for over ten minutes: "El mago de Tribilin, el mago de Tiribin . . ." ["The wizard of Tribilin, the wizard of Tiribin . . ."]

The therapist sings with him for ten minutes—a lovely melody, a song that children sing in Buenos Aires.

Then we sing another song, called *"La Vuelta Manzana"* ["All around the Block"].

P: Hurrah! Hurrah, Dr Rosenfeld! You sing with me, hurrah, Dr Rosenfeld! That was so good! The other therapist I had was always silent, sometimes for the 50 minutes of the session, totally silent, it was crazy.

A: How long were you with the psychologist?

P: I left right away, he didn't talk.

At another point in the session, the patient's way of being in the session is very strange—odd. His body is totally suspended in the air, held up in the following way: his head and nape of the neck are on the couch, and his feet, the heels, are on the desk. The rest is totally in the air, as if it were a plank supported at one end by the nape of the neck on the couch, and the heels of his feet at the other.

A: This is how you felt yesterday when you didn't have a session—alone and up in the air, with no support.

[The therapist remembered that he once had a schizophrenic patient who took this catatonic position and stayed that way for the entire hour.]

After a silence, Abelard tells me:

P: At the end of high school I had a psychotic episode, and they hospitalized me. My sister was 8 years old at that time. At that crazy time, I used to eat raw, hard rice. What could that mean?

A: You're swallowing the inedible things of life. . . . Not so much raw rice, but rocks, pains, abandonment, grandfather's murder, your parents' torture. . . . What else can you do sometimes but split your head into little pieces and spill it out? Because you can't stand so much pain.

P: The truth is, so much suffering. . . . Then we moved to another neighbourhood the subway got to . . . oh, no, it was another house . . . that was another house. . . . I got confused. You know? It was very hard when my Dad left home. . . .

A: Dad leaving you after so much suffering was like swallowing rocks, rice, you can't digest that . . . you can't swallow it.

P: *Che* . . . [Hey], doctor, you're right. Rocks . . . that's what I swallowed in life."

As he is leaving, the patient says, "This weekend I'd like to have a session. I need you. I need you." (pp. 15-16)

Their singing together occurred again and again, sessions that Rosenfeld describes as "an emotional communication such as I have seldom seen in my office: emotional communication through the aesthetics of music and poems" (p. 20). From a theoretical perspective, he relates these moments to the idea that the appearance of these children's songs, these lullabies, in the session with the analyst show how what is hidden or encapsulated can come out suddenly and be relived. This is not to be understood as regressive, but rather as the recovery in the psychoanalytic setting of what had been paralyzed and "encapsulated" since he was 18 months old—it is a reacquisition of parts of the self (p. 18). Rosenfeld also believes that in the fusion that is re-created in singing a duet, he and the patient recover the symbiosis with the parents that was broken off and shattered in his infancy.

Another patient, Lorenzo, 17 years old, was addicted to playing violent video games with characters that attacked, beat, and killed each other. He was hospitalized following an episode during which he broke all the furniture in his parents' house after his father tried to get him to stop playing his video game. On another occasion in a public arcade, unable to beat a video character that was attacking him, he broke the machine and the window of the arcade and needed to be restrained by the owners, who wanted to call the police.

In their first meeting, Rosenfeld asked Lorenzo what goes on in the video games, what he feels, and whether they arouse him. At this, the boy became enraged, stood up, and screamed at him: "This psychoanalyst is crazy! Look what he's telling me; he's talking about sex; he's mad, mad!" Rosenfeld formed the hypothesis that it was Lorenzo's own madness projected onto the mind of the therapist that was creating the anxiety. Lorenzo went on to say that the psychiatrists in the hospital confiscated his video game machine and forbade him to go near any others. Rosenfeld then had the thought that all the characters of Lorenzo's inner world were present on the screen, but they were projected onto an outer stage where he could murder them, or they could pursue him. He told the patient he would not forbid him to play his video games and, more over, that he wanted to play with him in order to understand him better, that they would be talking together, that he would gradually explain to him what was the matter, and that when he got a little better, they would go together to a video arcade. At this, Lorenzo said, " This doctor is mad, but I accept his treatment because at least he promises to go to the video games with me" (p. 120). He began seeing Rosenfeld four times a week.

Rosenfeld characterizes the early phase of Lorenzo's treatment as dominated by two features: a delusional belief in the reality of the characters and the violence that transpired on the video screen and his projection of these threats and dangers onto external objects, such as schoolmates, people on the street, and Rosenfeld himself, who Lorenzo feared would smash his head in and drive him crazy. The patient became paranoid and frankly delusional, fearing that his schoolmates were going to attack him with laser beams. He refused to go out into the street unless he could wear a protective suit. His mother made him an outfit of aluminum foil. Lorenzo said he felt protected against the laser beams. He continued seeing Rosenfeld every day, sometimes twice a day, including the weekend. He came to sessions dressed in his protective outfit and wanted to play the laser beam video with Rosenfeld. After losing one of these games to Rosenfeld, he told him, "Dr Rosenfeld, when you win, you can be transformed and become other characters, so even if I kill you now, you are still alive and have turned into another character" (p. 123).

Rosenfeld describes this communication as a key, a Rosetta stone, which enabled him to understand the dynamics of Lorenzo's projective process and the transference meaning of the delusion that he was being threatened and attacked. Rosenfeld realized that Lorenzo experiences him as someone transformed and projected into multiple and varied characters, that he is a dangerous, mutating object that becomes other objects, all pursuing him with laser beams. On the basis of these insights, Rosenfeld interpreted to the patient that when he, Rosenfeld, won the game, his character became a mutant and he was every other character in the video game. But since Lorenzo confused real life with fantasy, Rosenfeld pursued him not only through the characters on the screen, but also through hundreds of people in the real world. Rosenfeld claims that after interpreting in the transference the origin of the delusion, he was able to resolve the psychosis. Lorenzo went back to school.

Rosenfeld describes the course of Lorenzo's treatment in extensive detail. The overall progression can be summarized as moving from violence and delusions to the emerging ability to express hatred and anger against real objects in Lorenzo's life, such as his father and Rosenfeld himself. This is conceptualized as, first, a movement from the mindless enactment of symbolic rage to the verbal expression of conscious hate toward real external objects; second, a parallel recovery, or reintrojection, of internal objects; and lastly, a movement toward insight and the achievement of the depressive position (p. 133).

The most important link between Rosenfeld and modern psycho-analysis is the fundamental idea that treatment and therapeutic progression occur in the transference and that the analysis and management of the transference is the cornerstone of psychoanalytic treatment. "The chief secret of psychoanalysis, " he tells us,

> is that the work can be done in the transference. I consider a psychoanalyst as someone who thinks that everything the patient tells him is a message about his relationship to the therapist. This does not mean that interpretation must be going on all the time, at breakneck speed, or that everything has to be interpreted. But the message the patient is sending must usually be decoded with the right timing, in the here-and-now, including its known or strongly suspected genetic antecedents. (p. 113)

The second important link with modern psychoanalytic technique is the importance of studying and using the countertransference as a key to understanding what the patient is communicating in the moment and also as informing the analyst as to what, if anything, to say and when to say it. This is particularly important with psychotic, regressed, or other primitive patients whose total communication is most often indirect, symbolic, nonverbal, and, indeed, unconscious. As Rosenfeld explains,

> [I]n my view, the future of the investigation of psychotic or severely disturbed patients depends on two factors: first, the therapist's personal ability to contain the intense affects and emotions aroused by this type of patient, and, second, the detection and decoding of the messages the patient sends us via verbal means, non-verbal means, and communication systems of which we know very little as yet. These patients force us to experience intense emotions that they cannot feel or express in words. Our task as therapists is to decode these emotions in the course of supervision analysis or personal analysis in order to be able to adequately discriminate the personal aspects from what is projected or communicated by the patients through different means. (pp. 162-163)

This should resonate very powerfully with a modern analyst's understanding of the meaning and use of countertransference. In his last sentence, Rosenfeld also recognizes the importance of distinguishing what we call "objective" from "subjective" countertransference.

Rosenfeld differs from modern psychoanalysis in that he does not make use of the idea of a narcissistic transference or of an objectless state in his conceptualization of patients and in that he believes that interpretation is a means of resolving or reversing psychotic regressions, but only insofar as there is a healthy, non-psychotic part of the psyche to work with in the patient (p. 146). He distinguishes the psychotic from the neurotic transference on the basis of its greater intensity and of its delusional character: "*Psychotic transference* is the patient's total and absolute conviction about a delusional belief which he has concerning his therapist and—more important—acts out in consequence" (p. 229). It would be of interest to know whether and how Rosenfeld might find the concept of a narcissistic transference or of an objectless state useful in conceptualizing some of his patients, or some of his patients some of the time, and what implications this might have for his interpretive technique.

Rosenfeld is very good at showing how he creates a tailor-made psychoanalytic setting and a theoretical model for each patient, beginning from scratch and with very little presupposition as to what to expect, what to think, what to say, and what to do. Discussing the use of theory and models in conducting his work, he says that

> [W]e accept and use theories on the basis of our affects and our own life histories, and our infantile histories are probably as important as what we have learned from books and teachers. . . . Perhaps I have not learned from theories more than from my grandmother in order to construct a model and be able to listen to, understand, and think about a human being who is talking of his life and his feelings. I think my personal history determines the way in which I make use of my internal theoretical map. (p. 161)

In this book, Rosenfeld examines a wide range of severe pathologies and has something illuminating to say about each. In addition to the two cases described here, he provides a particularly insightful psychoanalytic classification of different types of drug addicts and discusses an eating disorder case and what he describes as a case of psychotic body image. Rosenfeld should be read as a model of a creative and intuitive master clinician who wants not only to heal his very disturbed patients, but has thought long and hard about how the conduct of psychoanalytic therapy can be used to achieve that aim.

Steven Poser

WORDS THAT TOUCH: A PSYCHOANALYST LEARNS TO SPEAK. Danielle Quinodoz. London and New York: Karnac, 2003. 209 pp.

In *Words that Touch: A Psychoanalyst Learns to Speak*, Swiss psychoanalyst Danielle Quinodoz focuses on emotional communication, presenting theoretical considerations as well as clinical case material and discussing her belief that psychoanalysis is a treatment modality that can benefit a diverse group of patients. One of her goals in writing this volume is to educate potential psychoanalytic patients and professionals in the viability of treatment. She contends that psychoanalysis is alive and well.

Quinodoz feels that prospective patients need to demonstrate an ability to use symbolism if they are to make the best use of psychoanalysis. Early analytic work may be geared toward the development of symbolic facility. Thus, patients who are initially unaware of the existence of an internal life may be helped to discover their psychic worlds, and hence symbolic capacity, through treatment. Quinodoz describes such patients as "heterogeneous," indicating that they may fluctuate between neurotic and psychotic aspects of their personalities. The inability to tolerate this heterogeneity often creates splitting within the psyche, causing an anxiety that for some individuals arouses a fear of madness. Failure to accept opposing feelings sometimes stirs patients to seek treatment as they struggle to ward off the prospect of losing an intact sense of self.

The book is replete with clinical illustrations. The author describes a 70-year-old patient, Berthe, who sought treatment due to depression derived from unfulfilled lifelong aspirations. Quinodoz initially questioned whether she could take such a patient into treatment. Following a failed liaison with her male analyst when she was 20, Berthe had had no further romantic encounters and had not married, nor conceived a child; she felt lethargic and unsatisfied. (This patient's first male analyst had overstepped the bounds of the professional relationship and engaged in an affair that ended badly.) The author wondered what would happen if the patient entered psychoanalysis only to realize it was far too late for many of these life-experiences to occur, despite the potential unfolding of her psychic life. Yet, Quinodoz thought that her own reluctance to treat the patient might be related to a countertransference feeling, and so she eventually entered into a treatment contract with Berthe. Many years after the treatment ended, the author encountered the patient at an exhibition. Berthe described a busy life in which she spent quality time with friends and had begun writing for a magazine. Berthe had come to life even though she had missed the opportunity to find a partner and create a family. At the age of 84, she was thriving as a consequence of developing a full internal life.

The author's fervent belief that psychoanalysis can open up endless possibilities for any patient who dares to think symbolically is second only to her passion for the analyst's need to "touch patients with words." Quinodoz works closely in the transference and continually evaluates her own feeling states. Following patient contact, she feeds her patients with their own words, making effective emotional interventions rather than intellectual interpretations. Always cognizant of the patients' defenses, their character structure, history, and the emotional climate in the room, Quinodoz attempts to "touch" patients with words that will permit them to "gain access to a whole network of associations" (p. 41).

Quinodoz addresses projective identification by reviewing the literature and examining its uses in treatment by various clinicians. Projective identification can stymie a case if the analyst is unaware of the power of this dynamic. Unlike projection, in which patients assign feelings to the analyst that the analyst is certain are coming from the patient, projective identification is more complex. Initially, the analyst simply has a feeling and believes it to be her own. If, on the other hand, the analyst is able to disentangle herself from the feeling and trace it back to the patient, there is potential for advancing the case. Many cases are wrought with obscure countertransference resistances based upon projective identifications undetected by the analyst. Quinodoz is keenly aware of the dangers of such dynamics in treatment. At the risk of experiencing her own madness, she is willing to go wherever her patients take her.

In order to help a patient reactivate the capacity to symbolize and to generate fantasy, Quinodoz says the analyst uses metaphor and imagery to jump-start the process. She describes a dream of her patient Elise in which a big wounded dog with a broken paw was being dragged by the current in a pool. Elise was certain the dog would die and that she should do something, but she did not know what to do. She recalled seeing a wounded dog on a trip she had once taken. While passers-by looked on indifferently, she wanted to ask for help but did not speak the language. The look in the dog's eye reminded her of her mother. She remembered that when vacationing as a little girl, she had noticed the current caused holes in the stream, forming whirlpools called "pots" that sucked things down. A dog once fell into such a hole. His owner dived in to save the dog, but both drowned (p. 38).

The author understood the dream and its associations as Elise's plea for help, along with an unconscious wish or fear to drag the analyst down into the swirling "pots" of her unconscious. During the session Quinodoz silently rehearsed interventions, unable to find the correct one until Elise spoke again and said coldly, "Analysis is just words; analysis is of no use." Quinodoz experienced a new set of feelings: she "felt swamped by a collapsing sensation" as if she were drowning in

one of the pots of the mountain stream. She believed Elise had unconsciously projected an anxiety-producing void in order to avoid feeling
it within herself. Assessing this situation, and her own countertransference feelings, she asked the patient, "Am I the pot?" The patient was
outraged by the seemingly bizarre question and asked for clarification.
Quinodoz continued, "Yes, the pot which might contain good things to
eat but instead is a hole sucking you down to the bottom of the stream
where you might go round and round until you drown" (p. 40). Elise
remained quiet for a few moments and then, with deep emotion, said,
"No one has ever sensed before that I really have a hole deep down
inside of me . . . a sadness [silence] . . . I think that's why I feel I am
looking after my mother out of duty as if she were still the presence of
an absence" (p. 41).

The author's words reached this patient through sensory and emotional routes. The multifaceted potential of the word "pot" implies both
nourishment and death, consumption and being consumed. As Spotnitz
(2004) has described, blocked pathways become available when a
patient is helped to put into words preoedipal conflicts that originated
in a period prior to the patient's acquisition of language. For these
patients, verbal explanations are useless.

This book is suggested reading for anyone wishing to enter the intimate space of the consulting room with a psychoanalyst whose clinical
techniques resonate with those of modern analysis. Quinodoz remains
in the moment with her patients as she strives to find interventions that
will reach each patient's madness and unlock the closed-off internal
self, speaking to the unconscious with *words that touch*.

REFERENCES

Spotnitz, H. (2004), *Modern Psychoanalysis of the Schizophrenic Patient.*
2nd ed. New York: YBK Publishers.

Barbara D'Amato

PRACTICAL PSYCHOANALYSIS FOR THERAPISTS AND PATIENTS. Owen Renik.
New York: Other Press, 2006. 179 pp.

Renik's book considers psychoanalysis as Freud thought of it, as
others re-interpreted it, and as Renik's empirical data, collected over
time from single-case studies, has shaped it. Not concerned with arguments, Renik speaks from his years of experience, saying what he

believes and illustrating it with cases. Renik is not advocating for an applied psychoanalysis here, but rather for the changes in analysis that he feels are needed due to its evolution. Take for instance Freud's original idea that the patient should come and talk rather than discharge in action. Having sex and making life changes were suspended for the relatively short time analysis lasted. According to Renik the trend toward longer analyses makes suspension of sex and life changes impractical these days.

Renik has long been looking at the changes in the work of analysis from the clinical perspective. Although his interest in the analyst's relationship with the patient places him in the relational school of thought, readers with a modern analytic background will agree with some of the modifications of technique he recommends, especially his idea that emotional experience rather than intellectual insight can promote cure.

Each chapter begins with a discussion of the theory or technique Renik is considering, and the remainder of the chapter is devoted to a case study. The chapters need not be read in order. Those familiar with Renik's writings may recognize some of the chapters from his papers of the 1990s (1995, 1996a, 1996b, 1997, 1998, 1999), following the relational surge prompted by Mitchell and Greenberg's (1983) book. Some cases, e.g., the boy with the bamboo phobia, come from work as far back as 1978.

Renik begins the book with a discussion of practical psychoanalysis, a phrase he feels is itself an oxymoron. He stresses that treatment should start with what the patient wants from treatment, for it is "the patient who must have the final word, because clinical analysis doesn't work when a patient is being treated for something the patient doesn't regard as a problem—even if the analyst is convinced that it is a problem" (p. 7). He discusses how the analyst can explore the patient's issues and points out that a "remedy has to be provided, as well. The patient has to be helped to find new ways of operating to put in place of the old, maladaptive ones" (p. 15). Renik calls into question purely intellectual insights that do not provide noticeable symptom relief.

After considering the beginning of treatment, Renik explores the intersection of theory and technique, again emphasizing a two-person psychoanalysis. The work of the analyst is difficult not because of what is known about the patient, but because of what is not known. Renik recommends a "collaborative working relationship between analyst and patient [that] is reciprocal, in the sense that not only does the analyst point out things to the patient about himself or herself of which the patient is unaware, but the patient points out things to the analyst about himself or herself of which the analyst is unaware" (p. 54). Neutrality, says Renik, is problematic. Even if the analyst tries, say by explaining the neutral stance to the analysand, he inevitably gives some comment that is less than neutral. As a result, the analyst has communicated "an atmosphere of hypocrisy." Renik adds that:

> Freud was especially concerned with the problem of untoward influence because he was at pains to distinguish clinical psychoanalysis from hypnotic suggestion and related treatment methods that achieve therapeutic results at the expense of the patient's self-determination. Accordingly, he recommended that analysts adopt a stance of *indifferenz* (literally indifference) when performing their clinical activities. *Indifferenz*, which came to be translated as *analytic neutrality*, has two aspects: the first is impartiality on the analyst's part with regard to the patient's conflicts, and the second is the analyst remaining, as far as possible, emotionally uninvolved in analytic work. . . . it's impossible for an analyst who is responsibly engaged in treatment not to be emotionally involved, and the analyst's emotional involvement invariably comes through to the patient. (pp. 73-74)

In one case example, Renik is asking his patient a question when the patient reports feeling he has lost the analyst's attention. The analysand, Ethan, associates this feeling to times his father would seem to turn from him, as if uninterested or impatient. Renik realizes that while he was asking the question, he had turned to check the answering machine, and the analysand had perceived the difference in the sound of his voice. Silently analyzing his own action, Renik comes up with the idea that his patient, a practicing medical doctor who was in the process of reporting on how he had successfully diagnosed and saved a patient, might have created a state in which the analyst felt inferior. Renik's next intervention is to admit to the patient that he had actually looked away, validating the patient's perception and apologizing. The admission, says Renik, helped Ethan to have a new feeling. "This is great," Ethan says, "I don't have to walk on eggs around you, worrying what's going to happen if you feel challenged. I wish I'd had this with my dad" (p. 87). Renik writes that another analyst with a different history would have different interactions in this situation, but for him, "my sadness at my mother's illness and death, my urges to rescue her, my rivalry with other rescuers, and a host of longstanding wishes, conflicts, and anxieties had been stirred up. I had not been conscious of any of these concerns" (p. 88).

For Renik, there are no patients who want to destroy their treatments, "only patients who *seem* to want to destroy their treatments" (p. 109). Freud's concept of the negative therapeutic reaction may aptly describe patients who don't feel worthy of their treatment, but Renik feels the concept is often extended to thinking that "a patient's failure to improve is motivated by aggression. . . . Invariably, the patient has another intention entirely in mind, which that analyst has failed to understand" (p. 110). Renik uses the case of Roger to illustrate this point: "Roger was never trying to destroy his treatment; he was only trying to feel safe. His motivation was not fundamentally aggressive. On the contrary, it was libidinal: in his own way, Roger was preserving the wishful image of a loving and lovable mother" (p. 115). Renik challenges the intention-consequence paradigm and comes close to saying that not every analyst is right for every analysand.

The book deals with some specific diagnoses like post-traumatic stress disorder, phobias, and panic. All psychological problems, from Renik's point of view, can be understood to represent post-traumatic stress of some kind. Even in cases of sudden onset, according to him, there is a fertile basis of trauma. Regarding phobias, Renik writes a chapter that uniquely compares desensitization techniques to analytic treatments. This chapter provides an interesting comparison of interventions that may look similar although they are based on different theoretical frameworks.

Other chapters reveal the author's practical approach. He talks about flexibility in couples work—e.g., seeing them individually as well as together—as more helpful than following the traditional rule that an analyst should not meet with the patient's significant other. In the final chapter, he makes the beautifully simple observation that he never terminates a patient; rather, he allows for interruptions of treatment and periods when patients go away. They come back when there are new goals, new benchmarks, or need for a booster shoot or inoculation.

The book presents a clear picture of how Renik works day to day, how he deviates from classical style, and how some of his modifications of technique are syntonic with some modern analytic ways of working even though his theoretical base is relational.

REFERENCES

Mitchell, S. & J. Greenberg (1983), *Object Relations In Psychoanalytic Theory.* Cambridge, MA: Harvard University Press.

Renik, O., P. Spielman, & J. Afterman (1978), Bamboo phobia in an eighteen-month-old boy. *Journal of the American Psychoanalytic Association*, 26:255-282.

Renik, O. (1995), The ideal of the anonymous analyst and the problem of self-disclosure. *Psychoanalytic Quarterly*, 64:466-495.

Renik, O. (1996a), The analyst's self-discovery. *Psychoanalytic Inquiry,* 16:390-400.

Renik, O. (1996b), The perils of neutrality. *Psychoanalytic Quarterly,* 65:495-517.

Renik, O. (1997), Conscious and unconscious use of the self. *Psychoanalytic Inquiry,* 17:5-12.

Renik, O. (1998), Getting real in analysis. *Psychoanalytic Quarterly,* 67:566-593.

Renik, O. (1999), Playing one's cards face up in analysis: an approach to the problem of self-disclosure. *Psychoanalytic Quarterly,* 68:521-539.

William Sharp

Books Received

Akhtar, Salman, ed. *Listening to Others: Developmental and Clinical Aspects of Empathy and Attunement*. Lanham, MD: Jason Aronson, 2007. 146 pp. softcover.

Boulanger, Chislaine. *Wounded by Reality: Understanding and Treating Adult Onset Trauma*. Malwah, NJ: The Analytic Press, 2007. 202 pp.

Burston, Daniel. *Erik Erickson and the American Psyche: Ego, Ethics, and Evolution*. Lanham, MD: Jason Aronson, 2007. 219 pp. softcover

Caligor, Eve, Otto F. Kernberg, & John F. Clarkin. *Handbook of Dynamic Psychotherapy for Higher Level Personality Pathology*. Washington D.C.: American Psychiatric Publishing, 2007. 272 pp.

Chasseguet-Smirgel, Janine. *The Body as Mirror of the World*. London: Free Association Books, 2005. 166 pp. softcover.

Fink, Bruce. *The Fundamentals of Psychoanalytic Technique: A Lacanian Approach for Practitioners*. New York: W. W. Norton, 2007. 304 pp.

Galton, Graeme. *Touch Papers: Dialogues on Touch in the Psychoanalytic Space*. London: Karnac, 2006. 194 pp. softcover.

Goldberg, Arnold. *Moral Stealth: How "Correct Behavior" Insinuates Itself into Psychotherapeutic Practice*. Chicago, IL: University of Chicago Press, 2007. 150 pp.

Husion, Kathleen, Susan B. Sherman, & Diana Siskind, eds. *Understanding Adoption: Clinical Work with Adults, Children, and Parents*. Lanham, MD: Jason Aronson, 2006. 259 pp. softcover.

Kernberg, Paulina, in collaboration with Bernadette Buhl-Nielsen & Lina Normandin. *Beyond the Reflection: The Role of Mirror Paradigm in Clinical Practice*. New York: Other Press, 2006. 211 pp. softcover.

Loewenthal, Del & David Winter. *What Is Psychotherapeutic Research?* London: Karnac, 2007. 348 pp. softcover.

Malan, David & Patricia Coughlin Della Selva. *Lives Transformed: A Revolutionary Method of Dynamic Psychotherapy*. London: Karnac, 2006. 343 pp.

Meissner, William W. *Time, Self, and Psychoanalysis*. Lanham, MD: Jason Aronson, 2007. 287 pp. softcover.

Oring, Elliott. *The Jokes of Sigmund Freud*. Third Edition. Lanham, MD: Jason Aronson, 2007. 168 pp. softcover.

Parens, Henri, Afaf Mahfouz, Stuart W. Twemlow, & David E Scharff, eds. *The Future of Prejudice: Psychoanalysis and the Prevention of Prejudice*. Lanham, MD: Jason Aronson, 2007. 325 pp. softcover.

Piers, Craig, John P. Muller, & Joseph Brent, eds. *Self-Organizing Complexity in Psychological Systems*. Lanham, MD: Jason Aronson, 2007. 192 pp. softcover.

Rangell, Leo. *The Road to Unity in Psychoanalytic Theory*. Lanham, MD: Jason Aronson, 2007. 133 pp.

Smadja, Claude. *The Psychosomatic Paradox*. London: Free Association Books, 2005. 233 pp. softcover.

Tucker, William. *How People Change: The Short Story as Case History*. New York: Other Press, 2007. 322 pp. softcover.

Wallin, David J. *Attachment in Psychotherapy*. New York: Guilford, 2007. 366 pp.

About the Authors

BERNSTEIN, JUNE, Ph.D., is Director of Public Information at the Center for Modern Psychoanalytic Studies, Dean of Students at the Boston Graduate School of Psychoanalysis, and co-editor of this journal. She is a faculty member, training analyst, and supervisor at both institutes and practices in New York City and Boston. She has published numerous articles.

CROWELL, MIMI G., Ph.D., is President of the Center for Modern Psychoanalytic Studies, where she also serves as a faculty member, training analyst, and supervisor. She is Program Director of the Boston Graduate School of Psychoanalysis-New York and on the editorial board of *Modern Psychoanalysis*. Dr. Crowell has written articles on psychoanalytic training, research, and supervision. She is a New York State licensed psychoanalyst in private practice in New York City.

GELTNER, PAUL, D.S.W., is the Director of Training at the Psychoanalytic Psychotherapy Study Center in New York City. He is also on the faculty of the Northern Rockies Institute for Psychoanalysis. He has published papers on dreams, child analysis, countertransference, and evolutionary psychology. The article in this journal is a selection from his upcoming book, *Emotional Communication in Psychoanalysis*. He is in private practice in New York City and in Brooklyn. His areas of focus include mood and learning disorders and individual and group supervision.

GOLDWATER, EUGENE, M.D., is a psychiatrist and psychoanalyst who practices in Hadley and Brookline, MA and teaches at the Boston Graduate School of Psychoanalysis in Brookline, MA and the Vermont

Graduate School of Psychoanalysis in Dummerston, VT. He has taught, lectured, and written about numerous subjects including fantasy and creativity, childhood and maturation, men and women, and sex and violence.

GOMOLIN, ROBIN POLLACK, Psy.D., received her B.S.W. from McGill University, and her M.A. in Psychoanalysis, Certificate in Psychoanalysis, and Psy.D. in the Study of Violence from the Boston Graduate School of Psychoanalysis (BGSP). She teaches at BGSP and in the Sociology Department at the University of Massachusetts, Boston.

HOLMES, LUCY, Ph.D, is a licensed psychoanalyst in private practice in New York City. A graduate of the Center for Modern Psychoanalytic Studies, she serves there as a faculty member and training analyst. She is President of the Society of Modern Psychoanalysts. Formerly Executive Director of the Center for Group Studies, she currently teaches in its Weekend Training Program. Author of numerous articles, many on women and women's groups, her article "The Object Within: Pregnancy as a Developmental Milestone," published in this journal, won the Gradiva Award of the National Association for the Advancement of Psychoanalysis as best article of 2002. Her book, *The Internal Triangle: New Theories of Female Development* will be out in December, 2007.

PIEMONT, LISA, Ph.D., is a certified psychoanalyst in private practice in Summit, New Jersey. She is a member of the faculty at The Academy of Clinical and Applied Psychoanalysis (ACAP) where she also serves as a fellow at the North Jersey Consultation Center, the clinical treatment service of ACAP.

Printed in the United States
91659LV00001B/1-249/A

9 780979 097287